POCKET GUIDE TO
TRACKS
AND
SIGNS

First published in 2014 by Bloomsbury Publishing Plc,
50 Bedford Square, London WC1 3DP

www.bloomsbury.com

ISBN 978-1-4729-0986-2

Bloomsbury Publishing, London, New Delhi, New York and Sydney

Bloomsbury is a trademark of Bloomsbury Publishing Plc

A CIP catalogue record for this book is available from the British Library.

Publisher: Nigel Redman
Project Editor: Jane Lawes
Design by: Rod Teasdale

Printed and bound in China by Toppan Leefung Printing Ltd

This book is produced using paper that is made from wood grown in
managed sustainable forests. It is natural, renewable and recyclable.
The logging and manufacturing processes conform to the
environmental regulation of the country of origin.

10 9 8 7 6 5 4 3 2 1

POCKET GUIDE TO
TRACKS
AND
SIGNS

Gerard Gorman

BLOOMSBURY
LONDON • NEW DELHI • NEW YORK • SYDNEY

CONTENTS

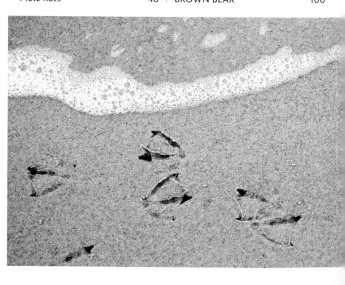

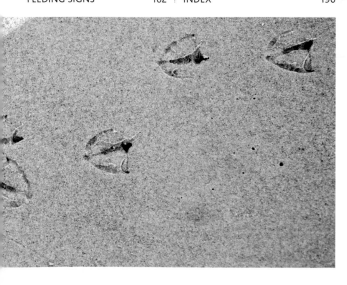

INTRODUCTION

My first encounters with wildlife took place in childhood in the UK, mainly along the Lancashire coast, the Mersey Estuary and in the Lake District, with the odd holiday to Shropshire thrown in. Then came school trips to the Peak District and Scotland, and though there were the usual 'teenage distractions' on those jaunts, I still managed to keep my eyes open to wildlife. For the last 25 years, I spent much of my outdoor time in continental Europe's woodlands and forests, particularly in central and eastern Europe, encountering wildlife that I could only read about as a child. In the 1990s, I focused on tracking down and observing the continent's woodpeckers in preparation for my handbook *Woodpeckers of Europe* (Bruce Coleman, 2004), and then my focus narrowed even further as I concentrated on a single species and subsequently wrote *The Black Woodpecker* (Lynx Edicions, 2011).

Woodpeckers, of course, are famed for their carpentry skills, excavating deep nesting chambers and foraging holes in trees, and I spent as much time examining these as I did the birds who made them, as I realised that they were of diagnostic use, indicating the presence of a particular species. But not all holes and marks in trees are made by woodpeckers; some are natural cavities and some are made by other wildlife, and I noted these as I came across them. Indeed, whilst searching and waiting for woodpeckers, I stumbled upon the tracks and signs of all kinds of wildlife – mammals, reptiles, insects, other birds – and I documented these, too. In fact, I began to actively seek out such evidence.

Some time later, while browsing through my photographs of droppings, tracks, food remains and even corpses, it occurred to me that my collection might interest others and so I decided to share them. The easiest way to do this was, of course, to use the Internet and thus my blog *Tracks and Signs* appeared. Clearly, there is great interest out there in this subject, as the blog soon caught the eye of other browsing wildlife enthusiasts, some of whom began to contribute with comments and photographs of their own. I hope this selection encourages you to head out along the shore and into the fields and forests in search of the wonderful wildlife that is waiting to be found.

Above: Foraging site of a Black Woodpecker *Dryocopus martius* on a fallen log in the Czech Republic. Europe's largest woodpecker is not afraid to drop to the ground to feed.

WHAT TO LOOK FOR

Animals leave all kinds of evidence that betrays their presence. Animal activity means that tracks, trails, prints, droppings, pellets, bones, gnawed bark, cracked nuts, split cones, burrows, dens, nests, dust baths, wallows, scent marking posts and corpses are all out there waiting to be found and examined. This book is an illustrated guide to the tracks and signs of the more common – as well as some of the more enigmatic – animals that can be found from the British Isles to the Mediterranean and eastern Europe. It is not a comprehensive guide to all the evidence that every European animal leaves – such a book is probably impossible to produce and any attempt would certainly mean a series of heavy volumes, such is the vastness of the subject matter.

Identifying tracks and signs is not an exact science. Factors such as weather, time and, for tracks, the quality and type of substrate can all hinder identification. Fresh Wild Boar or Grey Wolf footprints in crisp snow are not difficult to identify, but older prints, in melting snow, are quite another matter. The Wild Boar hoof-print can then easily be confused with that of a Red Deer and the Grey Wolf paw-print with that of a large sheepdog. The art of identifying tracks and signs is also somewhat neglected. Nevertheless, the tracking instinct definitely resides deep inside us – as anyone who has walked in the countryside with children will have seen. But like so many things within humankind today, it is dormant, lying largely unused. It is, however, easily awoken. There are innumerable types of tracks and signs in both urban and wilderness areas waiting to be found, examined and identified. Many will be very difficult, if not impossible, to assign to a particular species, but it is not necessary to live like an Indian scout or a Kalahari bushman to get involved. It is enough to simply be curious, aware and attentive.

Right: A hazelnut gnawed by Wood Mouse *Apodemus sylvaticus* or Yellow-necked Mouse *Apodemus flavicollis* in Hungary. A neat round hole on one side of the nut, surrounded by fine gnawing marks, is typical for both of these mice.

PRINTS

The best place to look for animal tracks is often on soft ground, after rain, or in mud, sand or snow. In the case of mammals, note first of all the type of footprint – paw, cloven-hoof or non-cloven-hoof (the latter meaning a horse, mule or donkey). Also observe the overall shape, main palm-pad size, the number and position of digits, whether there are any claw marks and the number of prints.

Below: A Wild Boar *Sus scrofa* hoof-print in soft mud in Slovakia.

Above: A European Otter *Lutra lutra* run in Hungary. Many animals inadvertently create clear paths as they travel to and fro, like this one through grass to the water's edge.

TRAILS

Many animals use regular routes as they go about their daily or nightly business. Most animals do not wander haphazardly, but rather follow favourite paths. This means that not only do they leave footprints, but also trails. The repeated use of such trails can result in them becoming worn and therefore easy to spot. Animals usually follow the easiest line through a given terrain, with barriers such as fallen logs, boulders, walls and water circumnavigated. Trails to drinking places will run to the waterside in open spots, rarely through thick vegetation, and paths through forests will generally avoid the understorey and scrub. Many species have learned to use convenient man-made routes such as footpaths, bridleways and logging roads to traverse difficult terrain, and this can also make things easier for the aspiring tracker.

DROPPINGS

Faeces are one of the most obvious indicators of animal presence. Some droppings are diagnostic, and finding them confirms that a certain species is present. The droppings of some animals even have special names: scat for dogs and cats, spraint for otter, guano for seabirds. Droppings come in all shapes and sizes: they can be straight, coiled, twisted, round, oval or disc-shaped; some animals leave single globular or tubular droppings, others piles of pellets or dung. This is a rather messy subject, but as a rule herbivores produce lots of neat round or oval droppings, whilst carnivores produce long, cylindrical ones that taper to a point. Droppings also vary in texture, being firm, sloppy or watery, depending upon what has been eaten and when they were excreted. Hard droppings are usually old, whilst soft droppings indicate a more recent event. Some animals scatter their droppings at random, others use regular latrines, some cover or bury them, whilst some species deliberately leave them in exposed and prominent places in order to signal their presence to potential mates and alert rivals to a claim on territory. Droppings can be prodded and broken with a stick to see what they contain. The contents – bones, skulls, chitin, feathers, fur, hair, fruit skins and stones – partly reveal an animal's diet. The colour and texture of droppings also supplies information – animals that have eaten berries will produce bluish, reddish or purplish excrement, while those that have swallowed bones may excrete white droppings.

Left: Piles of bat droppings accumulate below regularly used roosts, like this one of Serotine Bats *Eptesicus serotinus* in a church loft in Hungary.

DWELLINGS

Very few animals have a home which they use all year round; most only use a dwelling in the breeding period, though some also have places where they hibernate through the winter. Some animals sleep and raise their young in the open, but many use existing sheltered places such as tree holes, caves or even buildings. Others build their own dwellings. Some are just scrapes in the ground, or a few twigs or leaves placed on a ledge, or shell fragments pushed together on a beach. Some animals go further, digging complex systems of tunnels, whilst some birds tunnel into the ground or sandy banks.

Woodpeckers have taken excavation to another level, hacking cavities in trees, and these secure chambers are much prized by other wildlife that usurp them or move in once the woodpeckers have left. Many birds, and some small mammals, build nests. Nests can be elaborately woven cups, balls with an entrance hole or pennants that hang from trees. Many large birds construct sturdy platforms of twigs that are added to and grow in size each year. Whatever their design, most dwellings are diagnostic, meaning that their creators can be accurately identified.

Left: A Eurasian Badger *Meles meles* sett entrance with bedding outside being aired in England.

Below: This European Beaver *Castor fiber* lodge in Estonia is a sturdy, safe home.

WHERE AND WHEN TO LOOK

Things may often seem quiet in the countryside, but there is usually more wildlife about than we expect. Many species, whether mammals, birds or reptiles, are shy and have fled or hidden themselves by the time humans approach. Others only venture out after dark. But all wildlife leaves traces of its presence and activity behind in the form of tracks and signs. Some of the best and easiest places to look for this evidence are along watercourses, mudflats, sandy beaches, dunes, dusty trails, and man-made paths and roads, since mammals in particular will use these. Areas of mud, sand and snow are always worth examining. The best time to search is in the morning when nocturnal signs are still fresh and before the more ephemeral tracks disappear. Mornings after light rain or snow are

ideal. On a morning walk through a woodland in summer, it might seem as if nothing has moved there, but on a winter morning after overnight snowfall, it can be seen that this same woodland has been alive with nocturnal wildlife. Of course, many animals reside in the countryside, away from humankind, but rural settlements and even urban areas have their wildlife. In fact, some species have even become habituated to such places and their tracks and signs can be sought under our roofs and even on our doorsteps.

Below: One does not always have to head into the wild to see wildlife. For example, White Storks *Ciconia ciconia* often build their huge nests in settlements, like this one in Hungary.

MAMMALS

Mammals are a diverse group of animals that includes insectivores, ungulates, rodents, bats, lagomorphs and carnivores. Some are herbivores, others meat-eaters, and many are omnivores, eating whatever they can find: vegetable, animal, and even mineral. The smallest land mammal in Europe is an insectivore, the Pygmy White-toothed Shrew, which can be less than 4cm in body length. The largest is a herbivore, the European Bison, with mature bulls sometimes standing 2m tall at the shoulder. The smallest carnivore in Europe is the Weasel, with females sometimes just 15cm in body length, and the biggest is the Brown Bear, with old males often 1.5m at the shoulder when on all four paws and a good deal taller when stood on their back legs. Most of Europe's mammals are terrestrial, but some lead subterranean, aquatic, amphibious or aerial lives, and many move between these mediums. Some mammals are gregarious, with complex social systems and living in extended families. Some are loners, only willingly meeting others of their kind when they wish to breed. Most mammals are, with some justification, very wary of humans and are hard to track down and observe. Several are crepuscular, venturing out at dawn and dusk, and some are totally nocturnal – obviously the latter are particularly difficult to observe. Nevertheless, all the mammals of Europe leave tracks and signs, whether obvious or obscure.

Right: A Brown Bear *Ursus arctos* in Finland with the carcass of an Elk.

INSECTIVORES

The insectivores are an order of small mammals that is quite distinct from rodents, although they are sometimes presumed to be related. As the name suggests, insectivores mainly prey on insects (and invertebrates in general) rather than nibbling and gnawing vegetation. European insectivores include three very familiar families: hedgehogs, shrews and moles.

Below: A cluster of molehills in the Czech Republic. Groups or lines of soil mounds on the surface illustrate underground activity and tunnel arrangement.

Hedgehogs
Erinaceidae

There are three species of hedgehog in Europe: Western Hedgehog *Erinaceus europaeus* (Britain and western Europe), Eastern Hedgehog *Erinaceus concolor* (east and south-eastern Europe) and Algerian Hedgehog *Erinaceus algirus* (parts of Spain, southern France and the Balearics). The Western and Eastern are very similar in appearance – Eastern has a pale throat and chest, which contrasts with its dark belly. The tracks and signs of these species are largely identical.

DWELLING In colder regions hedgehogs hibernate in a nest (hibernaculum) built from grass and leaves that is usually hidden beneath a log or dense bush.

TRACKS Paw-prints recall a human hand, with five digits, though the smallest (the thumb) seldom leaves a mark. The rear paws are particularly long, with the toes closer together than on the forepaws. The long claws and toes show as one print in soft ground.

DROPPINGS Hedgehogs produce distinctive, dark, elongated, cylindrical faeces of 2–5cm long. They are usually shiny and brittle due to containing chitin fragments from insect exoskeletons, but they are sloppy when earthworms have been the main food. They generally have a rather bland odour.

Left: Hedgehogs are widespread, but their tracks and signs are not always obvious.

Right: Hedgehog droppings in Hungary. These examples are typical in shape, and in containing the shiny remains of insect prey.

Moles
Talpidae

There are at least three species of mole in Europe. The Blind Mole *Talpa caeca* occurs mainly in uplands in the southern Mediterranean, whilst the Roman Mole *Talpa romana* is found only in southern Italy. By far the most widespread is the Common Mole *Talpa europaea*, which ranges from Britain eastwards to Russia, though it is absent from Ireland and Scandinavia. The signs these species leave are very similar.

DWELLING Moles spend most of their lives below ground in a complex of tunnels, which they dig with their strong forepaws. Distinctive mounds of soil (molehills) are created above tunnel exits – there may be several molehills in a line or cluster. An exit hole can sometimes be seen in the centre of a molehill, and cylindrical, sausage-shaped sections of soil, which are the diameter of the tunnels below, may also lie on top. Long lines of earth ridges are formed when moles dig a tunnel just below ground level. These surface runs are formed by the tunnel roof having been pushed upwards.

TRACKS Footprints are rarely found, as moles spend so little time above ground, but trails that run between molehills are sometimes visible.

Left: Common Mole in England.

Right: New molehills (one in snow, one in turf) in the Czech Republic. In the spring, moles are active and burrow tunnels deep underground. These mounds of soil are thrown up at their exits.

Shrews
Soricidae

Shrews are one of the most frequently found dead mammals, often with no visible signs of predation. This is because these tiny creatures have a very high metabolic rate and must eat almost continually, hence many die from starvation. There are several species of shrew in Europe; the most widespread are the Common Shrew *Sorex araneus*, Pygmy Shrew *Sorex minutus* and Water Shrew *Neomys fodiens*, although the last is absent from Ireland and Iberia. The tiny Pygmy White-toothed Shrew *Suncus etruscus* (also known as the Etruscan Shrew) occurs in Iberia, southern France, Italy, the Adriatic coast of the Balkans and on some Mediterranean islands. It is the smallest mammal in Europe at 3.5cm long and weighing just 2.5g.

DWELLING Shrews build round nests with a simple hole entrance. They are made of straw, grass, moss or other vegetation and are placed under a tussock, log or stump, in dense undergrowth or inside an existing hole such as a mole tunnel. Unless the occupant is seen, most shrew nests are difficult to tell from those of voles. Water Shrews dig burrows, but most other shrews seldom do so.

TRACKS Shrews leave narrow runs through grass, leaf litter and surface soil, but these are hard to find and often indistinct. The tiny, long paws have five toes and claws – the forepaw is hand-like, the rear paw narrower. However, because shrews weigh so little, prints are seldom made.

DROPPINGS Droppings are small, pointed pellets, sometimes twisted and tapering at one end. They are blackish or grey when fresh, brown or paler when old, and they are brittle and crumbly, as they contain chitin from the exoskeletons of insects and often some cereal matter. Water Shrew droppings usually contain white crustacean fragments. The size depends on the species, with the smallest droppings being just 2mm long and the largest around 9-10mm. Droppings and prey remains are sometimes left in piles in runs, by nest entrances and on logs, stones and tussocks.

Right: Dead Water Shrew in England. The cause of death is unknown.

BATS
Chiroptera

About 45 species of bats (Chiroptera) are regularly found in Europe. With a body length of between 3.5 and 4.5cm long, the smallest is the Common Pipistrelle *Pipistrellus pipistrellus*, and the largest species is the Greater Noctule *Nyctalus lasiopterus*, which has a wingspan of up to 46cm. All bats leave conspicuous signs at their day-roosts, nurseries, migration stopovers and hibernation sites. Urine stains and droppings are the most obvious evidence of bat presence, but in many cases it is hard to assign these to an exact species, so habitat and location should always be considered.

DWELLING Some species of bat breed and roost in natural or old woodpecker holes in trees, clinging to the cavity walls. Others hang from walls and ceilings in caves, and walls, rafters and beams in buildings. Piles of droppings and urine stains below these locations betray them. Droppings may also be found glued to walls below the holes through which bats enter buildings. A greasy, brown body stain can mark where a bat has regularly squatted.

DROPPINGS Bat droppings are brown or black and usually less than 1cm (about the size of mouse droppings). They are rather dry and rough, consisting mostly of fragments of insects, and so crumble into powder when squeezed (fresh rodent droppings are moist, smooth and do not crumble, though they may do so when they are very old). Most bat droppings are not diagnostic to species, although size can narrow the number of potential species.

Right: Lesser Mouse-eared Bat *Myotis blythii* in Hungary surrounded by the fatty stain from its own body.

Following page: Schreiber's Bats *Miniopterus schreibersii* in Hungary. Undisturbed caves are used by many bats as day roosts. The bats only venture out at night to hunt.

Above: Huge amounts of bat droppings can pile up below large, regularly used roosts.

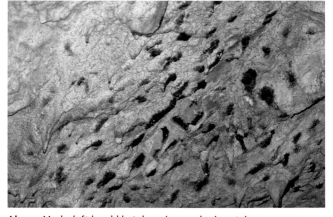

Above: Marks left by old bat droppings and urine stains on a cave wall in Hungary. It is hard to accurately identify which bats left these marks, but given the location, a cave-dwelling species such as Schreiber's Bat, Mediterranean Horseshoe Bat *Rhinolophus euryale*, Greater Mouse-eared Bat *Myotis myotis* or Lesser Mouse-eared Bat *Myotis blythii* is likely.

Above: Bat urine stains and droppings on wooden beams in an attic in Hungary.

Above: Serotine Bats *Eptesicus serotinus* crawling from their roost in Hungary. Droppings are stuck to the wall above.

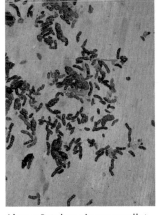

Above: Bat droppings are pellet-shaped and brittle, and easily crumble if handled. These are from Serotine Bats in Hungary.

RABBITS AND HARES
Lagomorpha

These well-known animals are not rodents as sometimes presumed, but belong to a distinct order of herbivores called lagomorphs. Rabbits and hares eat their own droppings (a process called refection) in order to digest them twice and so extract the maximum amount of nutrition.

Above: European Rabbits in England. These familiar mammals leave some easily identified signs.

Right: Rabbit burrow entrance in Spain. Several burrows will be concentrated in one area.

European Rabbit
Oryctolagus cuniculus

The European Rabbit is found mainly in western and southern Europe (it cannot tolerate the harsh winters of the very north and east). It is particularly common in Iberia and England.

DWELLING The rabbit is a social creature that lives in burrows. Where numbers of rabbits are high, extensive complexes of burrows and connecting tunnels called warrens develop. Entrances vary in size from 12 to 50cm in diameter. Larger burrow entrances with sand or earth on their doorstep might be confused with those of a fox; however, the entrance will be lower and rounder, and the strong odour that fox dens invariably emit will be lacking.

TRACKS Paw-prints are oval (forepaw: 2.5cm wide, 3.5cm long). The forepaws are smaller and rounder than the rear paws, which are elongated. Though rabbits have five toe-pads, only four usually show in prints. Paw-prints show claws and the overall print-shape is oval. Though less obvious, bare, scraped patches of ground, sometimes 10cm deep and often ringed by droppings, mark the edges of territories.

DROPPINGS Droppings are distinctive, being small, round and currant-sized (maximum 1cm in diameter). They are green, brown or black and moist when fresh, paler and dry when old, with fragments of grass apparent. When placed in tight piles (latrines), they are generally darker than when they are more scattered, as they are doused in urine and serve as territorial markers.

Left: Although rabbit numbers fluctuate greatly, they remain one of Europe's most familiar mammals.

Above: Fresh rabbit droppings are brown, black or green and moist. They are placed in piles in the open so that other rabbits can see and smell them. This is a small pile in England; regularly used spots are much larger.

Below: Old rabbit droppings are grey and dry. Some, such as these ones in Spain, resemble small pebbles.

Hares
Lepus

The Brown Hare *Lepus europaeus* (also known as the Common or European Hare) is widespread across Europe from Britain to Russia. The Mountain Hare *Lepus timidus* (also called the Blue or Tundra Hare) is smaller, with shorter legs and a white coat in winter, and is found in Ireland, Scotland, the Alps and Scandinavia. The two species overlap in several places, including northern England, Finland and the Baltic States.

DWELLING Hares do not dig burrows like rabbits (though Mountain Hares may usurp a burrow or dig under snow for shelter), but instead scrape a shallow depression, called a form, which is reused. This is often situated in an open field, sometimes under a shrub, and when in low vegetation may have a tunnel shape.

TRACKS Paw-prints are oval (forepaw: 3cm wide, 5cm long) and pointed at the front. Only four of the five toes and claws on the forepaw usually leave an impression; on hard ground only the claws will show. The soles of the paws are covered in fur, but signs of this rarely appear in prints. The trails of hares that have run at high speed (which is often) seem to show only two feet, as the hindpaws land on and cover the forepaws.

DROPPINGS Hare droppings are similar to those of rabbits, but larger (1–2cm in diameter), less round, flatter, disc-shaped and more likely to be in the middle of open fields. They are green, brown or black when fresh, straw-coloured when old, and placed in piles.

Left: Brown Hare in lowland Austria. Brown and Mountain Hares interbreed where their ranges overlap.

Above: Mountain Hare droppings in the Austrian Alps.

Right: Brown Hare paw-prints in the snow in Spain.

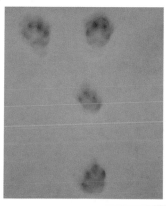

Below: Fresh, dark Brown Hare droppings in the snow in Spain.

RODENTS
Rodentia

Rodents are common. Indeed they constitute almost 40% of all mammals. All rodents gnaw and the tooth marks they leave on nuts, wood and vegetation can indicate their presence, although the animals themselves may not be seen. However, the gnawing marks of the smallest species are almost impossible to assign to a precise species. The largest rodent in Europe is the beaver and

the smallest rodents are mice. Rodents between these extremes include squirrels, hamsters, voles, rats and dormice.

Below: Beaver working on a log in Finland. No other rodent leaves such large, gnawing marks.

Red Squirrel
Sciurus vulgaris

Although rare in the British Isles, the Red Squirrel is quite common and widespread on the continent – in some countries it is even found in gardens and city parks. Not all Red Squirrels are red – a range of colour morphs occurs, including brown ones and almost totally black ones.

DWELLING Red Squirrels build nests of twigs and leaves in trees called dreys, but also den in tree holes, either natural or made by larger woodpeckers. Dreys are usually placed in the joint of two large branches or up against a tree trunk.

TRACKS Paws are elongated, with four long toes on the forepaws (2.5cm wide, 3.5cm long) and five on the even longer hindpaws (3.5cm wide, 4.5cm long). Two heel-pads often show on forepaw prints and the three palm-pads may appear as one single pad. Hindpaw prints show the three longest middle toes as the same length. When all four paws show in a track, the larger hind-prints are at the front, the smaller fore-prints at the back. The paw-prints of the Grey Squirrel *Sciurus carolinensis*, introduced from America into Britain and parts of Italy and now widespread, are slightly larger but otherwise difficult to separate.

DROPPINGS Squirrels tend to defecate at random, although piles of droppings will accumulate at regular feeding sites. Droppings are round, oval or pellet-shaped and 6–8mm in diameter.

Left: Red Squirrels vary in colour: this one has a brownish tail.

Above: Spruce cone gnawed by a Red Squirrel in Croatia.

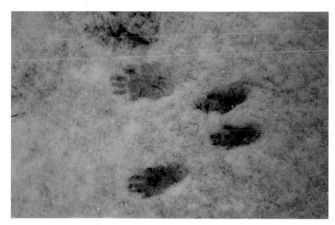

Above: Red Squirrel paw-prints in the snow in Hungary.

FEEDING SIGNS Conifer cones are systematically gnawed to remove the scales and extract the seeds. The core of the cone is usually stripped bare except for the very end, where the squirrel held the cone. Cones nibbled by Wood Mice look less ragged, almost completely shaved, as their nibbling method is neater. Squirrels often work on cones on the top of tree stumps, where piles of discarded cones and scales accumulate.

Susliks
Citellus

These ground-dwelling squirrels live in colonies on lowland, short-grazed pastures and bare grasslands. There are two species in Europe, Common Suslik *Citellus citellus* (east Austria, Hungary and the Balkans) and Spotted Suslik *Citellus suslicus* (south-east Poland, Ukraine and Russia). Both species hibernate through the winter.

DWELLING Susliks do not create significant mounds above their burrows (like mole rats and moles). Soil or sand is simply pushed out during digging and accumulates by the entrance. Old holes are not surrounded by excavation spoil. Though they live communally, most susliks (or a family when breeding) live in their own separate burrow, which has two or three entrances, at least one of which is a vertical shaft. Burrow entrances often seem too narrow for their owners to enter.

TRACKS Paw-prints are not often found, though they are sometimes left in sand around burrow entrances. Hindpaws are 3–4cm long.

Left: Common Suslik. In many areas this ground squirrel has suffered from inappropriate farming methods.

Right: A Common Suslik burrow in Hungary. Note the clear path from the entrance hole.

Dormice
Gliridae

There are four regular species of dormice in Europe: Garden Dormouse *Eliomys quercinus*, Forest Dormouse *Dryomys nitedula*, Edible Dormouse *Glis glis* and Hazel Dormouse *Muscardinus avellanarius* (also known as the Common Dormouse). The last is the smallest species and is fairly common in central and eastern Europe. The Edible Dormouse is the largest, also quite widespread and often found in urban areas, even hibernating in house lofts. The Garden Dormouse has a black facial mask and a tail that ends in a tuft. The Forest Dormouse is found in eastern Europe. Dormice hibernate from October to April in the north of Europe, but for a shorter period in the south.

DWELLING Dormice build summer nests of leaves woven together into a ball shape, with the entrance hole not always obvious. Nests for hibernation are simpler than those for breeding, the latter having a lining of moss, hair or feathers. Nests are usually in thick vegetation. When inside a tree hollow, woodpecker hole, wall cavity, nest box (intended for birds or placed out specifically for dormice) or burrow, the nest is less complex.

TRACKS Dormice are highly arboreal and rarely descend to the ground – the exception is Garden Dormouse, which will forage terrestrially. Dormice move around by using trees, hedgerows, buildings and wires, and so seldom leave tracks. Any prints that are found can be easily confused with those of the Red Squirrel, though they are much smaller. Forepaw prints are roughly 2 x 2cm, while hindpaw prints are 3cm long and 2.5cm wide. All paws have five toes, but the first toe on the forepaw is reduced and does not show in tracks. Claws rarely show.

FEEDING SIGNS: Gnawing marks on nuts and fruit are hard to separate from those of squirrels and mice.

Right: Edible Dormouse in Hungary. This nest in a specially designed nest box is a simple ball of oak leaves.

Above: Hazel or Common Dormouse.

Common Hamster
Cricetus cricetus

The Common Hamster is a bulky rodent – much bigger than the familiar pet Golden Hamster and more the size of a pet Guinea Pig. It is the most widespread hamster in Europe, though no longer common in the west. Its smaller relatives, the Romanian Hamster *Mesocricetus newtoni* and the Grey Hamster *Cricetus migratorius*, are found along the Black Sea coast in Bulgaria, Romania and the Ukraine. Hamsters live on lowland, dry, grassy and stony steppes and fields, feeding on seeds, roots, tubers and insects.

DWELLING Hamsters do not live in colonies. Males and females dig their own individual burrow system, which has several entrance holes but is not connected to those of other hamsters, though they may be located close by.

TRACKS All four paws have five long toes, but the first toe is tiny on the forepaw and does not show in tracks. Claw marks usually show on all paw-prints. Both fore- and hind-paws are narrow, but the hindpaws are much longer.

DROPPINGS Faeces are small, dark, rough, pellet-shaped and about the size of a grain of rice.

Left: Common Hamster.

Right: Unfortunately, Common Hamsters, like this one in Hungary, are more likely to be found dead – after being hit by vehicles or mangled by agricultural machinery – than seen alive.

Above: Common Hamster emerging from burrow.

Mole Rats
Spalacinae

If it were not for the signs they leave, mole rats would go largely unnoticed. They are one of Europe's most mysterious mammals, being blind, subterranean and nocturnal. They are also rare, their steppe and grassland habitat having for centuries been degraded, ploughed up or planted with trees, and in some areas they are regarded as pests by farmers because of their tunnelling habits. Until recently two species were thought to live in Europe: the Greater Mole Rat *Spalax microphthalmus* (from Romania eastwards) and the smaller Lesser Mole Rat *Nannospalax leucodon* (in lowlands in Hungary, Serbia, Romania and Bulgaria); however, recent studies suggest that other genetically distinct species may exist.

DWELLING The most conspicuous sign that mole rats leave are the mounds they make when throwing out earth whilst digging tunnels. Mounds are four or five times bigger than those of true moles (which are not related) and run in lines or clusters.

Above: Mole Rat in the Ukraine. These mammals are rarely seen above the ground like this.

48

Above: A cluster of mole rat mounds in Serbia.

Above: A mole rat mound in Serbia, with a mobile phone for size comparison.

Voles
Arvicolinae

Europe is home to many different vole species. The most widespread include the Bank Vole *Clethrionomys glareolus*, the Northern Water Vole *Arvicola terrestris*, the Field Vole *Microtus agrestis* and the Common Vole *Microtus arvalis*, although the last is absent from the British Isles and the Mediterranean. There are several other rarer, more localised species in Europe. The tracks and signs of most voles are very similar.

DWELLING Voles make a ball-shaped nest of grass and other vegetation placed in a burrow in the ground, a tussock or a bank. Though not truly colonial, the burrows of land-dwelling voles may be clustered together. There is no clear mound, but soil debris may lie around burrow entrances. After snow has melted, the maze of narrow surface runs that linked the entrances become evident. Entrance holes to the burrows of Water Voles can be below the water line.

TRACKS Due to the similarity of the prints of the various vole and mice species, location and habitat is important when attempting to identify tracks. Voles have long paw-prints, with four toes on the forepaws and five on the rear. Rear paws are longer than forepaws, but in contrast to rats and mice, this difference is not always obvious. In soft surfaces, such as wet mud, the toes are clearly splayed.

DROPPINGS Vole droppings vary between 8 and 12mm long and are smooth, pellet-like and rounded at both ends (rat droppings are slightly bigger and not as rounded). They are placed in open latrines, sometimes in piles, and serve as territorial markers.

Left: Water Vole in England.

Above: Tracks of Northern Water Vole in mud in Hungary. Only the four-toed front paws (about 2cm long) are clear in these tracks. Note that there are no tail drag marks, which is typical.

OTHER SIGNS Tubular lines of soil, which lie in winding patterns on the ground in spring, are the work of Water Voles. These earth patterns result from tunnels, which the voles made under snow, becoming filled with soil that then remains and keeps the tunnel shape after the snow has melted.

Right: Northern Water Vole earth patterns in Estonia.

Mice
Murinae

The most widespread mice in Europe are the House Mouse *Mus musculus*, the Harvest Mouse *Micromys minutus*, the Wood Mouse *Apodemus sylvaticus* and the Yellow-necked Mouse *Apodemus flavicollis*. All of these species occur from Britain eastwards across the continent to Russia. The Striped Field Mouse *Apodemus agrarius* is widespread in central and eastern Europe. The Steppe Mouse *Mus spicilegus*, which looks very much like a House Mouse, is common in the grasslands and farmlands of south-east Europe.

DWELLINGS House Mice build nests in attics, basements, cupboards, sheds, barns, under floorboards and between sacks and walls. Materials used include straw and shredded paper and cloth. Rural mice use grass, hay and other vegetation.

TRACKS Hindpaw prints show five toes, but the forepaw prints show four, as the fifth toe is small and rarely makes a mark. Rear paws are noticeably longer than forepaws. Given the general abundance of mice, the frequency of finding their paw-prints is actually rather low. This is because mice are so small that their body weight seldom makes an impression in substrates. In addition, mice often jump rather than walk.

DROPPINGS Mouse droppings are pellet-shaped – the size of rice grains. Colour depends upon what has been eaten: urban mice droppings are generally darker than those of rural mice, which eat more vegetation and hence void paler, greener droppings. They are moist when fresh

Left: A foraging Harvest Mouse.

Above: A food storage mound of Steppe Mouse in Serbia. This species digs an extensive burrow complex with conspicuous food stores on the surface that can hold many kilograms of grain.

and harder when old; the similar-sized droppings of small bats are dry and crumble into dust when squeezed. House Mice have favourite spots where piles of droppings, urine and food remains build up, although a scattering of droppings also typically lines runs.

Right: House Mouse droppings in Hungary.

Rats
Murinae

Both the Black Rat *Rattus rattus* (also called Roof or Ship Rat) and the Brown Rat *Rattus norvegicus* (also known as Sewer or Norway Rat) colonised Europe – and indeed most of the world – from Asia. They are now firmly established as abundant natives wherever there are people. Rats are social animals that live in colonies, breed prolifically and are generally regarded as pests.

DWELLING Black Rats do not dig burrows, but use existing cavities inside buildings: under floorboards, in pipes, and between walls, insulation, boxes and sacks. Brown Rats that live indoors do the same, whilst those outdoors dig communal tunnel systems with entrances of between 5 and 10cm in diameter. When burrows are made in the ground, often on a bank, the spoil is simply piled up outside the entrance, but there is no mound proper. Holes are used as food stores and breeding sites. Nests are placed within holes and made from straw, hay, shredded paper, string, cloth or whatever is available locally.

TRACKS Rats move along regular routes, usually near or under some form of cover. Clear paw-prints show four toes on the forepaws and five on the hindpaws. As with mice, rear paws are longer than forepaws. Indoors, the tail can leave a long, thin line in dust, flour or fine grain. Greasy, brown body smears on beams, floorboards and walls also indicate regular runs.

Above: The Brown Rat is a common urban mammal.

Above: Fresh Brown Rat droppings in Hungary. Note that they are moist and there is a urine stain on the doormat.

DROPPINGS Brown Rat droppings are typically blunt-ended, rod-shaped pellets of around 1cm long. Black Rat droppings are slightly smaller and usually more scattered but otherwise very similar. When fresh, droppings are shiny and putty-like, becoming harder and drier over time. Rats use regular latrines to void, and large piles of droppings can accumulate, but they also urinate when on the move and sprinkled stains betray regular trails.

Above: Old Brown Rat droppings in Hungary. Note that they and the surroundings are dry.

Beavers
Castoridae

Two species of beaver are found in Europe: the native European Beaver *Castor fiber* and the introduced Canadian Beaver *Castor canadensis* (also known as the North American Beaver). In Finland, for example, probably only Canadian Beavers occurs. Beavers are the largest rodents in Europe with a body length of 75–100cm, and are mostly nocturnal, but they leave obvious and unmistakable signs of their presence. These signs are all but the same for both species and include dams, lodges, felled trees, woodchips, stripped bark, tooth marks on trees and scent mounds. Occasionally, beavers are killed by large trees that do not fall in the direction intended when felled.

DWELLING Beavers are famed for their construction skills. Lodges and dams are built from branches, sticks, earth, mud and vegetation, all impressively packed and woven together to form solid structures. Lodges are sturdy, 1–3m high, constructed on land or in water and with a hidden, underwater entrance. There are differences in style: some beavers build tidy-looking lodges with every stick seemingly placed precisely, whilst other lodges seem to have been hastily assembled. Some beavers dig burrows in banks rather than build lodges. Dams stem flowing water, creating ponds where beavers can then forage on trees in the flooded area. Waterside trees are felled in such a way that they fall across the stream or channel to help dam it. Dams can be over 100m wide, but are usually much smaller and placed in a series, blocking streams or channels. The smallest dams can be overlooked when they resemble piles of washed-up debris.

Left: European Beaver in Sweden.

Right: A beaver dam creating a pond in the Czech Republic.

Above: A beaver dam across a canal in the Czech Republic.

Previous page: A beaver lodge under construction in Finland. Note the fresh earth and sticks on the lodge and the piles of recently cut twigs and saplings nearby.

 TRACKS The rear paws are large (14–15cm long and 9-10cm wide) and show five toes and short claws. In soft surfaces, the webbing between the toes also leaves a mark. Forepaw prints are much smaller (around 5cm long and 4cm wide on adults) and usually show four toes with long claws, though there are actually five toes, but no webbing. Small trees felled further away are repeatedly dragged along conspicuous narrow trails to the lodge or dam. These trails are usually muddy, but the beaver's flat, broad tail often wipes away any paw-prints as it is dragged along.

Above: A beaver path in Poland. The wet mud indicates that this trail is active.

DROPPINGS Beaver droppings are not easy to find, as they are often released in water and soon disintegrate. They are tubular or globular, brownish, composed of vegetation and fibrous.

FEEDING SIGNS The most obvious foraging signs are teeth marks on felled or standing trees – softwood species such as alder, aspen, birch, willow and poplar are chosen rather than conifers. When fresh, the gnawed area of timber is clean and pale; when old it is dark. On standing trees, gnawing marks are low down on the trunk – under 1m high – as beavers do not climb. When saplings are gnawed and break off, the stump tip resembles a sharp stake.

Above: A tree freshly gnawed by beaver in Estonia. Deciduous trees are preferred.

Above: The exposed dark wood and lack of fresh, light woodchips on the ground show that this is old work by a beaver.

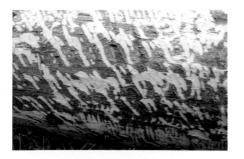

Left: A log with the tooth marks of a beaver in Poland.

DOGS
Canidae

Four species of wild dog are found in Europe: Red Fox *Vulpes vulpes*, Arctic Fox *Alopex lagopus*, Golden Jackal *Canis aureus* and Grey Wolf *Canis lupus*. The tracks and signs these wild carnivores leave can easily be mistaken for those of pets or stray dogs, and in some cases they are so similar that certain identification is unsafe. There are so many breeds of dog, from the tiny to the huge, that there is almost always one that overlaps in size with a wild relative.

Below: The Grey Wolf is a noble but much-maligned animal.

Right: A dog dropping in England. This Golden Retriever dropping is large – the size of a wolf's – but it is sloppy and lacks hair, fur and other contents that wolf droppings typically contain. Location is crucial. Such droppings in urban areas are unlikely to be those of wild animals.

Red Fox
Vulpes vulpes

The fox is one of the most widespread and familiar carnivores in Europe. Though mainly inhabiting open or lightly wooded country, in the British Isles it has become an increasingly urban animal, even living in the heart of some cities.

DWELLING Foxes dig a den or earth, with a narrow, high entrance. There are typically several entrances/exits, each fronted by a widely spread pile of excavation debris. There is usually a strong smell and often some scat, hairs and food remains by occupied earths. Tracks and signs of both foxes and badgers by an earth mean that both animals are using the site – a not unusual occurrence. Urban foxes will use holes under and in buildings, pipes, tree roots and even in piles of rubble.

TRACKS The paw-prints can easily be confused with those of domestic dogs of a similar size, but they are generally narrower, with the front two pads clearly spaced ahead of the hind pads and an open space at the centre of the print. The four short toes all show claw marks. The palm-pad is not significantly larger than the toe pads, unlike in most domestic dogs. Fox trails usually follow a straight, narrow track-line, unlike the wandering trail of dogs.

Left: The most common wild canid in Europe is an intelligent predator.

Right: A fox earth in a sandy bank in Hungary. Note the narrow but high entrance and the spread of dug-out sandy soil.

Above: A fox dropping in Spain. White droppings are common and indicate that a large number of bones have been eaten.

DROPPINGS Though essentially a carnivore, foxes will eat most things including carrion, household scraps, berries, even grass, and this is reflected in the colour and texture of their scat. It is usually long, thin and twisted at one end, and varies in colour from brown to purple to white. It is invariably firmer and less sloppy than that of domestic dogs (which consume canned dog food), contains food fragments and sometimes lies in several pieces. However, urban foxes that have eaten household scraps and perhaps even dog food produce scat more like pet dogs. Scat is placed in obvious places such as on open paths and atop stones, tussocks and molehills, to mark territory. Fresh droppings and urine emit a strong odour.

OTHER SIGNS When foxes kill a bird, the feathers are bitten off, not plucked out. Thus, the feather shafts are square near the end. This contrasts with feathers from a bird killed by a hawk, which will lie plucked with their pointed quill ends intact.

Right: Fox droppings on a tree stump in England. Foxes often leave their scat in prominent places as territorial markers. Note the fur content.

Below: Lapwing *Vanellus vanellus* feathers from a fox kill in Hungary. Note that the ends of the quills are blunt, as they have been bitten through.

Grey Wolf
Canis lupus

The Grey Wolf is the largest wild dog in Europe (indeed in the world) and the second largest carnivore in Europe after the Brown Bear. Size varies depending upon factors such as genetics, food and climate – as a rule, wolves in the north are larger than those in the south. Within all populations males are larger than females. Most adults are 1–1.5m long from the tip of the nose to the tip of the tail, which makes up one-third of the total length. After a long decline in Europe, wolves seem to be increasing in range and number, although they are still often misunderstood and persecuted. The population remains fragmented (in most of western Europe they remain scarce), but they can be found in parts of Iberia, the Alps, the Apennines, the Balkans, Poland, the Baltic States, Scandinavia and Finland. The largest numbers live further east in Russia and its former states, but Romania's Carpathians is the European stronghold with around 3,000–4,000 individuals estimated (40% of the European population outside Russia). Wolves were lost from Britain in the 1700s. There are core wilderness areas where wolves reside, but they are great wanderers, often moving at night, and so their tracks and signs are occasionally found in urban areas. In central and south-east Europe, tracks of the Golden Jackal could be confused with those of a wolf. Golden Jackals are smaller and slimmer than a wolf,

with shorter legs and more prominent ears. Most adults are about 1m from the nose to the tip of the tail, with a golden or light brown coat. Though essentially a carnivore and a top predator that hunts for deer and Wild Boar, wolves also take rodents, ground-dwelling birds and insects, and rob smaller predators of their prey. Wolves regularly scavenge for food, take carrion and, like most dogs, also eat some vegetable matter. In some areas, domestic stock is also taken.

Left: Grey Wolf.

Above: A wolf paw-print in frozen ground in Spain.

Above: A wolf paw-print in the snow in Finland.

TRACKS Wolf prints are very similar to but larger and broader than those of all but the biggest domestic dogs. Key things to note include long toe-pads, which are well spaced out and splayed apart, and long, pronounced claws that leave clear marks. Four toes clearly show and the overall shape of the print is oval. Location is important – clearly, large canine prints outside regions where wolves are known to exist are likely to be those of domestic dogs. Care should also be taken in identifying tracks in those areas, such as the Carpathians, where large sheepdogs are kept to deter the local wolves. Wolves usually trot but sometimes lope along. When hunting, they run. The track-line of a wolf is rather narrow and often straight, whereas most domestic dogs walk in a wandering zigzag.

DROPPINGS Wolf scat usually contains hair and grass; its colour depends upon what has been eaten and how fresh it is. It is dropped in obvious places, such as the middle of paths or on tussocks, to mark and announce territory. Scat found in areas where there are large domestic or feral dogs or sheepdogs can be difficult to identify to species.

Above: Fresh wolf scat in Poland. The wet nature of the dropping indicates it is recent, and the fur and hair content are typical.

Above: This wolf scat is providing a feast of nutrients for these butterflies at Aggtelek, Hungary. Note the size and firmness of the droppings and the hair content.

MUSTELIDS
Mustelidae

This family of small carnivores includes the Stoat, Weasels, mink, polecats, martens, badger, Wolverine and otter. The smallest is the Weasel, the largest the Wolverine, but whatever their size, all are expert, voracious predators and some are infamous for the foul-smelling odour they spray when threatened. Despite some species being widespread and rather

common, mustelids can be elusive and count amongst the least studied of Europe's mammals.

Below: Wolverine *Gulo gulo* in the snow in Finland. The large paws of this northern hunter function as excellent snowshoes.

Weasel and Stoat
Mustela

The smallest carnivore in Europe is the Weasel *Mustela nivalis*, with some females in Scandinavia (a race called Least or Snow Weasel) having a body length of just 15cm. The Stoat *Mustela erminea* (also called the Ermine) is slightly bigger, with a longer black-tipped tail. In the north and east of Europe, both species moult their reddish-brown summer coat to white in the winter.

DWELLING Dens are made in holes in root systems, walls, banks, or burrows usurped from rabbits, and lined with fur from their prey.

TRACKS Stoat and Weasel paw-prints are not easy to find. They have five toes with claws, with the forepaws leaving an overall oval print and the hindpaws a longer shape. Stoat fore-prints are about 2cm long and 1.5cm wide, whereas the hind-prints are 3.5cm long and 1.3cm wide. The main pads are lined with fur in winter, but this only shows in the clearest prints. In snow, an imprint of the body may connect the paw-prints. Weasel prints are very similar to the Stoat's, but smaller.

DROPPINGS Stoat droppings are long (4–6cm), thin and twisted at one end. Rodent hair, feathers and fur and bone fragments are often visible. Weasel droppings are similar but much thinner and shorter, resembling a piece of twisted wire. Both species will pile up droppings in their dens, but also place them in prominent places, on walls, stones and logs, as territorial signals to others.

Left top: Weasel.

Left bottom: Stoat.

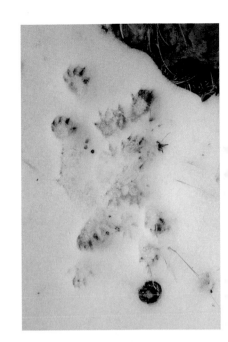

Right: Stoat paw-prints in the snow in Spain.

Below: A fresh Stoat dropping on a log in Austria.

Mink and Polecats
Mustela and Vormela

There are two species of mink in Europe (the native European Mink *Mustela lutreola* and the introduced American Mink *Mustela vison*) and three species of polecat – the European Polecat *Mustela putorius*, the Steppe Polecat *Mustela eversmanni* and the Marbled Polecat *Vormela peregusna*. The latter two species are found in the east of Europe. The tracks and signs of both mink and polecats are similar and can only be separated in the best of conditions. The European Mink is critically endangered, having vanished from much of its former range due to over-trapping, habitat loss and competition from its larger and dominant American cousin. They hold on in the Danube Delta in Romania and Ukraine, and in Latvia, Estonia, Belarus, northern Spain and south-west France. European mink are often difficult to see, as besides being rare they are mainly nocturnal. They are seemingly nervous, agile, amphibious mammals that swim and dive well (being able to remain underwater for up to two minutes), with long, slim bodies, a fairly short tail, short legs, relatively large heads and short ears. Typical adult males are around 55–60cm in length, including the tail, whilst females are shorter. The coat is glossy, blackish-brownish, and the chin and lips are white. Most American Mink lack white on the upper lip.

Above: European Polecat; sometimes called Western Polecat.

Right: European Mink tracks in Spain. Any sightings of this endangered animal should be treasured. Twenty cent Euro coin for comparison.

DWELLING Mink live by freshwater lakes, rivers, streams, canals and marshes, using existing holes and burrows as dens. Steppe and Marbled Polecats live on dry lowland grasslands and will usurp and enlarge existing animal burrows.

TRACKS The paw-prints of all the above species have five toes, but the print of the forepaws often only shows four. The overall shape of the paw-print is round. The kidney-shaped palm-pad and toe-prints are well spaced out and in wet mud form a star-like shape. Claw marks are usually visible but sometimes merge with the toe-pads, forming teardrop shapes. Mink have webbing between the toes, particularly on the hind-paws, and this may leave a trace in wet mud or firm snow.

DROPPINGS Droppings of mink and polecats are similar, though those of polecats lack aquatic prey remains. They are typically 5–6cm long and 6–9mm in diameter, twisted, tapered at one end or pellet-shaped, and blackish when fresh, with bone, feather, shell and insect-case fragments. Mink hunt both on land and in water for small mammals, birds, frogs, molluscs, crayfish, fish and insects; polecats rarely hunt by water. Mink usually void in the open near water, for example on a log, stone or low wall.

Left: American Mink, coming out of a burrow.

Right: European Mink droppings in Spain. As the droppings of both mink are so similar, location is important to note.

Martens
Martes

There are two species of marten in Europe – the coniferous forest-dwelling Pine Marten *Martes martes* and the Beech (or Stone) Marten *Martes foina*, which is much more likely to be seen in open broadleaved woodlands and urban areas. Pine Martens have a cream-yellow bib, whereas Beech Martens have a white bib and also differ in having a longer tail, less densely furred paws and more rounded, shorter and more widely spaced ears. Both species are roughly the size of a pet cat – around 50cm in body length – with a bushy tail of about 25cm. Martens are more arboreal than polecats.

DWELLINGS Martens den amongst rocks and in holes in cliffs and trees. On the continent, Pine Martens often use Black Woodpecker holes and Red Squirrel dreys. Beech Martens are more likely to use attics in both abandoned and occupied houses, sheds, barns and garages. In such places mysterious damage to insulation, electrical wiring and pipes can be the work of Beech Martens.

 TRACKS Marten tracks are not easy to find, as the animals tend to avoid mud and the Pine Marten in particular is often in trees. There are five toes on each paw, though the fifth toe is often indistinct in tracks. The palm-pad has four lobes, but it also often

Left: Pine Marten.

Right: Martens will leave their droppings in prominent places as a visual signal to others, as shown by these droppings found in Hungary.

fails to leave an impression, although the heel-pad of the forepaw can leave a mark. The overall shape of the print is fairly round, usually 3cm wide and up to 4cm long in adults, though if the whole main pad shows, it can be 5cm x 6cm. Though martens have strong claws, these may not show well in prints, as they are semi-retractable, except in firm mud or snow. The feet are well furred in the Pine Marten and in snow this may create a misleadingly large print.

DROPPINGS Martens are mainly nocturnal and carnivorous, preying on voles, mice, squirrels, rabbits, birds, frogs and insects, but readily eat carrion and some fruit, berries and mushrooms. Droppings are placed in prominent places such as on stones, logs, the middle of paths and, in the case of Beech Martens, on man-made structures such as steps, roofs, drain covers and even car bonnets. Droppings are variable in size but usually long (1–1.8cm) and thin, cylindrical and often twisted or coiled. Undigested hair, feathers, eggshells and fruit skins and stones are often visible. Beech Marten droppings can also contain undigested household scraps. The droppings of both martens are sweeter-smelling than those of other mustelids. Marten droppings vary in colour depending on diet but are usually black when fresh and purple or red after the consumption of cherries.

OTHER SIGNS Beech Martens will sleep under the bonnets of parked cars, especially in winter when the warmth from an engine is no doubt welcome. Such individuals leave scraps of food, droppings and urine stains and chew on cables and insulation.

Left: Beech Marten in the snow.

Above: Martens that have eaten berries have red or purple droppings, such as these in Hungary.

Below: Beech Marten dead on a road. Living in close proximity to humans and their cars has its own risks.

European Otter
Lutra lutra

Widely distributed and locally not uncommon across Europe, the European Otter (also called the River Otter) is semi-aquatic. It is rather wary and mostly nocturnal, thus tracks and signs are more likely to be found than the actual animal. Adult otters can be 1m long from the snout to the tip of the tail, with male (dog) otters bigger than females.

DWELLING A den (called a holt) is dug in a waterside bank, sometimes between the roots of an overhanging tree. The entrance is usually safely below the waterline and so hard to find.

TRACKS Otters have webbed paws with five digits. The overall shape of the forepaw print is round (6cm wide and 6.5cm long), and the hindpaw is more oval (6cm wide and up to 9cm long). Often only four of the five toes on each foot leave an impression. Otters have sharp claws, but they do not always show well in prints or they merge with the toe-pad to form a teardrop shape. In snow or mud, the trail of the dragged tail is often visible, and in wet mud the print of the webbing between the digits may show. Otters use regular pathways down banks through vegetation into water, which are called slides, and are often obvious.

DROPPINGS Spraint is placed in the open, often in prominent places near water such as on boulders, sluice gates or by bridges. It is black, slimy or damp when fresh, sometimes just a tarry, liquid smear, but it is pale, dry and brittle when old. It is thin, varying in length from 3 to 10cm. Typical contents are fish bones, scales and crustacean fragments, sometimes fur and feathers, and it has a fishy but not unpleasant odour.

Above: Otter prints in wet mud in Hungary. In most of the prints, only four toe-pads can be seen.

Right: An otter print in dry mud in Hungary. In this print, all five toe-pads can be seen, although the outer and inner toes are faint.

Far left: European Otter walking on ice.

Eurasian Badger
Meles meles

Badgers are stocky and strong, with small heads, thick necks, short tails and stout legs. They prefer broadleaved woodlands with clearings, and open country with copses, though mixed and coniferous forests, scrubland and urban areas are also occupied. Badgers are crepuscular and nocturnal, emerging at dusk to forage.

DWELLING Badgers live in communal underground dens with tunnels and chambers, called setts. There can be up to 10 entrances, spaced 10–20m apart. Entrance holes are lower and wider than those of fox earths and there is usually a deep, furrowed path before the entrance. Piles of earth and discarded bedding also betray sett locations. Sometimes foxes will use part of an active badger sett, and at such times tracks and signs of both species will coincide. Badgers use regular routes through their territories, though they may be indirect with haphazard patterns. Vegetation on these trails is flattened by the animal's low, heavy body.

Above: Eurasian Badger: an often unreasonably persecuted mammal.

Above: An old entrance to a badger sett in Hungary. Note the lack of fresh earth and the dry leaves in and around the hole. Although this entrance is not in use, the sett below may still be occupied, but accessed via other holes.

Right: A badger pathway under a deer fence in Serbia. There were no clear paw-prints or claw marks in the dry, sandy soil, but a tuft of light fur on the wire revealed the species responsible.

Above: Badger paw-prints in mud in Hungary, showing clear claw marks.

TRACKS Badger paw-prints are distinctive. They have five toes on each paw, with elongated, non-retractable claws that show in prints – though the inner toe may not show. The toes are positioned in a row above a broad, kidney-shaped palm-pad. The forepaws are bigger than the hindpaws and have longer claws that leave clear marks.

DROPPINGS Badgers are versatile and opportunistic foragers, with an omnivorous diet that includes fruit, vegetables, nuts, bulbs, tubers, acorns, cereals, earthworms, wasp and bee grubs, eggs and carrion. Live mammal prey includes moles, hedgehogs and rabbits. Badger droppings reflect this varied diet, being sausage-shaped or rounded, dry or wet, solid or runny, and often littered with seeds, cherry stones, insect parts and bones. Droppings are deposited in shallow, open, uncovered dung-pits (latrines) in the ground, away from the sett, but also on open ground. Droppings often have a strong, musky odour.

Above: A badger latrine in Hungary.

Above: A badger dropping with beetle wing-cases and berries in England.

Wolverine

Gulo gulo

This much-misunderstood animal is often considered to be vicious and dangerous, but in reality Wolverines are very wary, invariably fleeing at the first sight, sound or smell of humans. A stocky, powerful animal, low-set on short legs, with a broad head and small ears and eyes, the Wolverine resembles a large badger. Males are around 1m long and up to 45cm high at the shoulder. The paws are large, with five toes and large claws. Wolverines are mainly scavengers searching for carrion, but they also hunt for live mammal prey such as beavers, smaller rodents, young deer and Elk, or adults that are wounded or hindered by deep snow. Outside the breeding season, Wolverines are loners, residing in the wilder parts of Scandinavia, Finland and Russia. Given its behaviour and the remote places it inhabits, there is much more chance of finding the tracks and signs of a Wolverine than seeing this magnificent animal itself.

DWELLING Females raise their kits in a den, in a cave or under or between rocks or logs.

Above: A Wolverine at a Reindeer carcass in Finland.

Above: Wolverine and Red Fox trails crossing each other in the snow in Finland.

TRACKS Once found, paw-prints are usually unmistakable. The most likely confusion species are Grey Wolf and lynx when tracks are in a set of four, or Pine Marten when in a set of two. The overall shape of the print is oval, but can become triangular when spread in snow. The paw-prints are large and much bigger than those of any of its relatives. The hindpaws are 14–19cm long and 6–9cm wide, the forepaws 11–14cm long and 6–9cm wide, but again the print may be much wider when the paws are spread. There are five digits on each paw, but the fifth toe may not show on the front paw-print and the heel-pad may not show on the hindpaw print. Claw marks and foot-drag are usually evident, and in mud or snow an imprint of fur may show. Wolverines have a very particular gait, bounding along, seemingly erratically, as if bouncing on springs. This produces a unique 1–2–1 offset pattern of paw placement with the middle print made by two paws overlapping.

CATS
Felidae

Europe is home to three species of wild feline: Wildcat *Felis silvestris*, Eurasian Lynx *Lynx lynx* and Iberian Lynx *Lynx pardinus*, the last also known as the Pardel Lynx. All are shy, elusive, largely solitary, nocturnal hunters. As cats have retractable claws, which they draw into their paws when walking, their tracks rarely show clear claw marks, whereas those of both wild and domestic dogs almost always do.

Below: The Wildcat is one of Europe's most elusive mammals. This one was photographed in Spain.

Eurasian Lynx
Lynx lynx

The lynx is Europe's largest cat, with adults ranging between 80 and 130cm in length from the nose to the tip of their short tail, and standing 55–75cm at the shoulder. Lynx are found in scattered, often isolated populations in southern, central and eastern Europe, the Balkans and Fennoscandia. They have disappeared from most of western Europe, although reintroduction projects in France, Switzerland, Slovenia, Italy, Austria, Germany and the Czech Republic are proving successful. Lynx vanished from Britain around 500AD. The smaller Iberian Lynx occurs in parts of Portugal and Spain. Lynx live mainly in forests with good numbers of deer and boar, or mountains with Chamois, though hares and grouse are also preyed upon. For most of their lives lynx are loners and, except for chance encounters, are only betrayed by the tracks and signs they leave. Even in areas where they are more numerous than wolves or bears, lynx are still usually harder to find.

DWELLING The female raises her kittens in a cave, under a crag, between rocks or in the hole of another mammal such as a badger.

TRACKS With the exception of prints in snow, lynx leave few signs. As with all cats, the overall shape of the paw-print is round (in dogs it is oval) and the main pad makes up about half of the whole print. Lynx tracks are large (around 10cm long, which is three times bigger than the average tabby – thus this is the safest way to rule out a domestic or feral cat) and the foot functions as a snow-shoe. As with other felines, the four short toes

have retractable claws that seldom make marks. In mud or snow an imprint of dense fur may be evident around and between the pad and between the toes. Lynx walk in a narrow track-line, but often meander, with hind- and fore-prints often overlapping.

Left: Eurasian Lynx.

Right: Lynx paw-print in light snow in Hungary. There are no claw marks and a larger round area beyond the print marks, caused by the furry pad, is just visible.

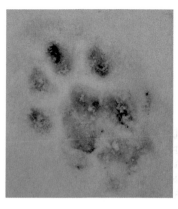

Below: Lynx scat in Slovakia. Though not buried – probably because of the frozen soil – this dropping has been partly covered in snow.

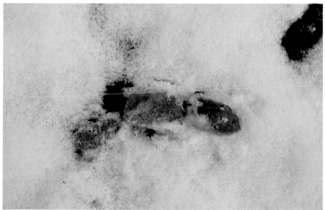

DROPPINGS Lynx scat is similar to that of a domestic cat, but much longer (20–25cm) and fatter. It is not easy to find, as it is often buried.

OTHER SIGNS Like all cats, lynx scratch tree trunks, leaving claw marks. Males also urinate on scenting posts (trees and rocks) to inform females of their presence and to mark territory. Large prey is dragged to a secluded spot, partially eaten and then hidden under logs or rocks or in leaf litter or snow. Carcasses of larger prey, such as Roe Deer or Chamois, will show bites to the neck, not the hindquarters.

Wildcat
Felis silvestris

The Wildcat is the ancestor of the pet cat and the two are so closely related that when they meet and mate, they produce fertile offspring. In fact, hybrids between Wildcats and domestic or feral cats are widespread across Europe. The tracks and signs of Wildcats and other cats are almost identical. Wildcats are marked much like a domestic tabby, but are bigger, being 50–75cm long, with a thick tail of up to 35cm in length.

DWELLING Females raise their kittens in a cave, a crevice amongst rocks, under exposed tree roots, in a tree hole, in dense vegetation or in abandoned fox, badger or rabbit holes.

TRACKS Wildcat paw-prints are difficult to separate from those of domestic and feral cats. They are on average bigger, but there is overlap so caution should be exercised with tracks found near settlements and in areas with known feral cat populations. The overall paw-print shape is round. Paws have five toes, but only four usually show and the main pad has three lobes. The claws do not leave marks.

DROPPINGS Wildcat scat is black or brown when fresh, sometimes greenish, and paler when old. It is long, cylindrical, tapered at one end and usually broken into segments linked by hairs. It often contains bones, fur, feathers and grass. Some scat is buried, but it is also placed in exposed spots, such as on stones, logs or in the middle of paths at the edges of a territory, to serve as a visual marker to rivals.

OTHER SIGNS Scratches on trees, like other cats.

Left: Scottish Wildcat.

Above: A Wildcat trail in fresh snow in Hungary. The clear, deep holes are where the rear paws were placed on top of the forepaws. Due to the depth of the snow, the animal was walking slowly and thus some prints were not placed on top of others.

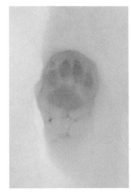

Right: A Wildcat paw-print in Hungary. Note the lack of claw marks that is typical for all cats.

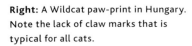

COMMON GENET
Genetta genetta

The Common Genet (also known as the European or Small-spotted Genet) is a mostly nocturnal predator. Although not uncommon, they are solitary, shy and elusive. In some ways genets resemble a long-tailed cat, but they are more closely related to mongooses. They are found in southern France, Spain, the Balearic Islands and Portugal. Populations of escaped animals are reported to survive in Germany and Belgium. Genets live in open woodlands, often with rocky features and water bodies, but also in olive groves, orchards and even urban areas. They are expert tree climbers, preying mainly on small mammals, birds, eggs, lizards, insects and some fruit. Adults are between 40 and 55cm in length, with a further 40–50cm of tail.

TRACKS Genets have an overall round print of about 3.5 x 3.5cm. A three-lobed main pad leaves a blunt triangle shape. Four toes show and the claws may or may not leave marks.

DROPPINGS Regular latrines are used and located in prominent places such as on, or by, rocks, walls and gutters. Droppings are long and cat-like.

Above: Common Genet at night.

Left: The paw-prints of a Common Genet in Spain. Note the lack of claw marks here, which might suggest a cat. A 20 cent Euro coin has been included for size comparison.

BROWN BEAR
Ursus arctos

Although it can be regarded as Europe's largest carnivore, the Brown Bear actually has an omnivorous diet and some individuals are mainly vegetarian. Most of Europe's bears are found in Russia, though they also occur in smaller numbers in the wilder parts of Scandinavia, Finland, the Baltic States, Spain, Italy, Austria, Slovenia, the Balkans, and the Carpathians in Slovakia, Poland, Romania and the Ukraine. Brown Bears vanished from Britain around 500AD.

Right: A Brown Bear walking across a swamp in Finland.

Below: A Brown Bear's den dug into a slope in Finland.

Above: Claw marks are usually obvious in bear prints, though not in the case of this forepaw print seen in Poland.

Above: The forepaw print of a Brown Bear in Finland. The print is broad and a clear ridge can be seen between the toes and the main pad.

TRACKS Most Brown Bear prints are easy to identify. Each paw has five large toe-pads in a row. The long claws leave clear marks and there is usually a clear ridge between the row of toe-pad prints and the main paw-pad. Forepaw prints are shorter and broader than the rear ones, and wider than they are long, whereas the hindpaws are longer and narrower. Fore-prints suggest a huge badger, hind-prints perhaps a human foot. Small bears, in particular, leave hind-prints that might suggest those left by a bare-footed man, although the innermost toe on a bear is very small and short (on a human it is the biggest toe). The biggest, mature male bears leave fore-prints of around 28cm long and 20cm wide and hind-prints that are 30cm long and 18cm wide.

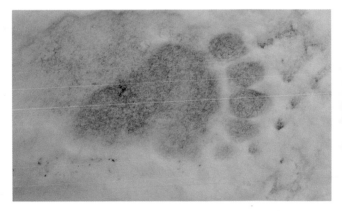

Above: A Brown Bear hindpaw print in snow in Slovakia.

Right: A Brown Bear forepaw print in snow in Slovakia.

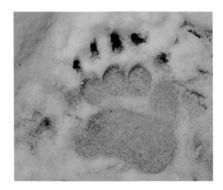

DROPPINGS Besides fresh meat from kills, bears feast on carrion, rob prey from other predators, dig for grubs and earthworms and raid bee and wasp nests for honey. In some regions bears visit rubbish dumps, ski-resort waste bins and settlements to scavenge for scraps. Bears preparing for winter hibernation fatten up on acorns, nuts, beechmast, berries and windfall fruit. In spring, bulbs, tubers, grass, roots and honey are sought. All this means that bear droppings vary a great deal in colour, consistency and content. They often contain undigested vegetable matter. Bears that have fed upon masses of ripe berries void sloppy, reddish or bluish droppings, and those that have eaten carrion or ungulate prey produce firmer brown ones. Droppings are often placed in a pile and may be globular, sausage-shaped or a single mass.

Above: Fresh Brown Bear droppings in Poland. Note the author's 44 (11 UK) size boot for comparison. This dropping was rather pale and upon close inspection was found to contain much seed and grain. This bear had been eating feed placed out for game.

Above: Brown Bear droppings in snow in Slovakia. Note the bird tracks around the dropping.

Above: Brown Bear droppings vary in colour according to what has been recently eaten. The bear that left this in Slovakia had been eating berries, hence the purple colour.

OTHER SIGNS Bears are aggressively territorial, but conflicts are largely avoided by dominant individuals leaving signs, such as scratches on trees and piles of droppings, that inform intruders of who is in charge locally.

Above: Claw marks on a tree in Poland. Bears probably scratch trees for several reasons, including making a visual signal for other bears to notice. At the same time, this cleans and sharpens their claws and perhaps releases a little tension.

Right: Male bears will reach up and snap off the tops of thin trees, such as this one in Finland, to make territorial statements. This shows rivals how big, tall and strong they are.

CLOVEN-HOOFED MAMMALS
Artiodactyla

Cloven-hoofed mammals have four digits: two cleaves (at the front) and two dew claws (at the rear). In Europe, they include deer, Chamois, bison and Wild Boar. Of course, domestic cattle, sheep and goats are also cloven-hoofed, but horses, mules and donkeys have non-cloven-hooves – in fact, there are no wild mammals in Europe with the latter hoof type. Most deer leave

two cleave marks, but Reindeer, Elk and also Wild Boar leave four imprints. This is because the dew claws of these animals are located low down on the leg, which means they touch the ground.

Below: The woodland-dwelling European Bison, such as this one in Poland, has come back from the brink of extinction.

WILD BOAR
Sus scrofa

The Wild Boar is Europe's only member of the pig and peccary family. These robust animals are common and widespread on the continent, though not always easy to observe, as they are wary, being a game species, and mainly nocturnal. Many populations are maintained for hunting and fed in hard winters to ensure good numbers survive to the spring.

DWELLING Resting places are difficult to separate from those of large deer, being merely depressions in vegetation. Droppings, hair or nearby hoof-prints help seal identification.

TRACKS The hoof-print of the Wild Boar almost always shows four imprints, two broad slots at the front and two round holes at the rear made by the dew claws. Only domestic pigs leave similar prints, though Reindeer, Elk and sometimes Roe Deer also show dew claw marks. The widest part of the print (up to 7.5cm on adult boars) is at the rear between the two points made by the dew claws. Hoof-prints made by young boars are narrower and pointed at the front, while those of adult boars are broader and more rounded.

Above: An adult male Wild Boar in winter.

Above and below: Wild Boar hoof-prints in Hungary. The marks of the dew claws are clear in both wet mud and melting snow.

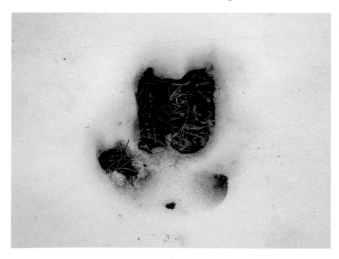

Above: Wild Boar droppings in Hungary.

DROPPINGS Wild Boar are omnivores, eating anything and everything from acorns, nuts, tubers and crops to small rodents, earthworms, grubs and carrion. Wild Boar droppings look very much like those of farm pigs, so location is important. Colour and consistency varies according to what has been eaten. They are usually cylinder-shaped, with disc-shaped sections fused together, or like dumplings.

OTHER SIGNS Wild Boars regularly wallow in mudbaths. Red Deer also create wallows, but those of boars are usually in clearings and more open places, while deer prefer more secluded spots in forests. Hoof-prints and droppings around wallows are often the best way to identify exactly who uses them. One of the most obvious signs left by Wild Boar is a patch of disturbed, rutted, rooted-up ground. This foraging method, called rooting, is usually done at night. It is simply the act of digging for food (tubers, truffles, worms, etc.) with the snout and tusks. Sometimes the ground is turned up as if done with a spade or roughly ploughed. Rooting sites are found in both open country and within forests and can be the work of one boar or several. They can cover a small patch of ground or be extensive, and in a given area there are usually several rooted patches. Rooting and grubbing up of the soil is beneficial for woodland biodiversity.

Above: A Wild Boar rooting site in the Czech Republic.

Above: A Wild Boar wallow in Slovakia.

EUROPEAN BISON
Bison bonasus

The European Bison (also called the Wisent) is Europe's heaviest land mammal; adult bulls can weigh over 800kg. Both cows and bulls have horns. Unlike their famous American cousins that live on open prairies, these huge animals inhabit mature, wet, broadleaved forests with secluded glades where, despite their size, they can hide away with surprising ease. The main wild populations reside in the old-growth forests of eastern Poland and Belarus.

DWELLING Large areas of flattened grass show where herds or lone bulls have rested. These can be distinguished from those of larger deer and Wild Boar by size and the presence of hair, dung and hoof-prints.

Above: Bull European Bison in winter.

Above: Bison hoof-print in Poland, with a ballpoint pen for size comparison.

TRACKS Bison have cloven hooves. Prints are very large, broad and can only be confused with those of domestic cattle (though beware of those of Elk that have not left clear dew claw marks). The location of prints is important and caution should be exercised in areas where cattle are present. Though bison have four toes, only the two main cleaves are developed and leave marks. The rear two dew claws are placed high on the hind foot and rarely touch the ground, though they may leave marks in deep snow or mud. The cleaves are rounded at their tips, convex at the rear and concave at the front. A high ridge of soil or other substrate is usually left between the cleaves. Hoof-print size depends upon the sex and age of the animal.

Above: A fresh, wet, bison 'cow-pat' type dropping in Poland.

Above: Bison hair in Poland. An animal has rubbed against this stump leaving a mass of distinctive reddish hair.

Above: Bison rubbing post in Poland. These huge animals are unable to scratch themselves, so they rub themselves against trees. This post is smooth, so it is obviously regularly used, and there are signs that it has also been gnawed.

DROPPINGS Bison dung is a large, round, wet, brown pat when fresh, and paler and dried with a crust when old. Piles of dung can resemble a plate of burnt chocolate pancakes.

OTHER SIGNS Bison leave conspicuous wallows in muddy, forest clearings. In the rutting season, bulls churn up turf and soil with their hooves and horns. Clumps of brown-reddish hair can be found in spring when bison moult.

CHAMOIS
Rupicapra rupicapra

Mountain goats of steep, rocky places and meadows, Chamois are found high in the Alps, Pyrenees, Apennines, Carpathians and the Balkan ranges. Some authorities regard the different European populations as composed of distinct separate species. Chamois reach 130cm in length and stand 75–80cm high.

TRACKS The hoof-prints of adults measure around 6cm long and 3.5cm wide, with two clearly separated parallel slots of even width. The dew claws rarely leave marks. Most prints are found in the winter in snow, and rarely in the summer, as they frequent largely inaccessible and rocky ground.

DROPPINGS Chamois deposit round or oval black droppings about 1.5cm in diameter. They are moist when fresh and often fuse together in piles.

Above: Chamois are found in Europe's highest mountain ranges.

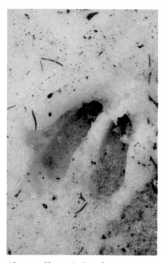

Above: Chamois hoof-prints in the snow in Spain.

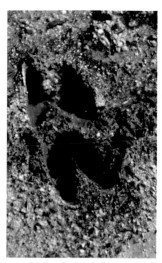

Above: Chamois hoof-prints in gravel in Austria.

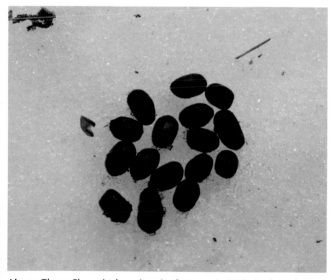

Above: These Chamois droppings in the snow in Spain look much like those of a domestic goat, so location is important to note.

DEER
Cervidae

There are five native species of deer in Europe and several alien, introduced species such as the Muntjac, Sika and Chinese Water Deer. Deer hoof-prints have two long slots that are pointed at the front (whereas sheep slots are rounded). As deer ruminate and vegetation is finely digested, their droppings are usually

black and shiny with no plant fragments visible and it is difficult to tell those of different species apart except by size.

Below: Elk bull with huge palmate antlers in Finland.

Red Deer
Cervus elaphus

In the British Isles, Red Deer inhabit open moorland or parkland, but on the European continent they are forest animals that are bigger and heavier and the stags have more impressive antlers. Red Deer live in mixed forests with glades and clearings where they graze and also strip tree bark – spruce is a favourite. At dusk they will move out into more open areas to feed.

TRACKS Hoof-prints are large (7cm wide and 9cm long) – only Elk has bigger hooves. They are broad, with the cleaves being narrower at the front and having a wider gap than at the rear. The dew claws rarely leave a mark, as they are placed high up the leg and do not touch the ground.

DROPPINGS There are two basic types of droppings, both dropped at random in loose piles and with no distinct smell. The oval, cylindrical pellets, indented at one end, are typically 2–3cm long and 1.5cm thick, bigger than those of Roe Deer but smaller than Elk's, though there is overlap. The second type is a single

Above: Red Deer stag.

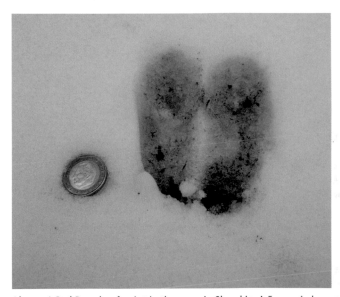

Above: A Red Deer hoof-print in the snow in Slovakia. A Euro coin has been included for size comparison.

Above: Red Deer pellet-like droppings in Austria.

123

Above: A Red Deer dumpling-like dropping, with pellet types in the background, in Austria.

lump, a dumpling-like mass formed by sections fused together. All droppings are glossy black and soft when fresh, but brown-green within, and changing to brown and dry when old. There are no obvious food fragments.

OTHER SIGNS Deer thrash bushes and saplings with their antlers in order to rid themselves of loose velvet. This is called fraying and results in battered and broken vegetation at forest edges and in clearings. Red Deer fray in late summer. Bark is nibbled and stripped from trees as food and across most of Europe any signs of this above 2m high will be the work of Red Deer.

Left: A Red Deer gnawing post in Austria.

Right: A sapling frayed by Red Deer in Hungary.

Roe Deer
Capreolus capreolus

Roe Deer are Europe's smallest native deer species. Bucks and does are generally similar in size, standing 60–70cm at the shoulder. They are widespread in lowlands from Britain eastwards to Russia, and in woodlands and farmlands with copses, so are often easy to observe. In many countries populations are managed and fed in winter to ensure high hunting bags.

TRACKS Hoof-prints are clearly smaller (3cm wide and 4.5cm long) than those of Red Deer and show pointed slots. Dew claw marks often show when the ground surface is soft and the weight of the deer has fallen on the rear of the feet and the hooves are splayed.

Above: Roe Deer are the most common deer of open country in Europe.

Right: Roe Deer hoof-prints in dry soil in the Czech Republic. Note the very narrow and pointed shape of the cleaves.

DROPPINGS Roe Deer droppings are typically oval or pellet-shaped, pointed at one end and left in piles. They are smaller than those of Red Deer and similar in size to those of goats. They lack odour, are glossy black and moist when fresh, and brown and dry when old.

OTHER SIGNS Bucks mark territory by making shallow scrapes on the ground, rubbing trees with scent from glands on the face and scraping bark from saplings with their antlers. All deer strip off tree bark (barking) to eat it and also gnaw at the wood beneath. Roe Deer mainly fray bushes in spring, but being smaller and having smaller antlers, this is often not as obvious as that done by Red Deer.

Above: Roe Deer droppings in the Czech Republic. In areas with other deer species, the size of droppings helps with correct identification. These are bean-sized and about 1.2cm long.

Right: Tree barked by Roe Deer in Hungary. It is hard to say for certain which species barked this tree, but the height of the barking, quite low down, suggests Roe Deer.

Fallow Deer
Dama dama

Though locally common in much of Britain and the continent, many populations of Fallow Deer are reintroduced and now feral or farmed.

TRACKS Two long and narrow slots usually show, with the dew claws only leaving marks in very soft surfaces. The outer edges of the slots may be straight or concave. Male hoof-prints are typically 8cm long and 5cm wide, very much like those of smaller Red Deer. In Britain and a few places on the continent, the hoof-prints of introduced Sika Deer *Cervus nippon* can also be mistaken for Fallow. The prints of the female are smaller.

DROPPINGS Separating Fallow Deer droppings from those of Red Deer can be tricky. They are smaller than those of most Red Deer stags, but overlap in size with younger Red Deer. Fallow Deer droppings are also pellet-shaped, with one end pointed and the other indented, glossy black when fresh and with no obvious food fragments. They are usually dropped in small piles in the open or on tracks. Single or several fused blobs are dropped in summer.

Above: Three Fallow Deer hinds.

Above: A tree barked by Fallow Deer in Hungary. Barking by this species is all but impossible to tell from other deer of similar size.

OTHER SIGNS As with other deer, tree bark is eaten in winter when other food is sparse, leaving distinct teeth marks. Bucks mark territory by urinating in scrapes, thrashing vegetation and saplings, and wallowing in mud.

Reindeer
Rangifer tarandus

Reindeer are found from Lapland (in Norway, Sweden and Finland) eastwards into Siberia. Many animals on the tundra are domesticated and managed, though wild populations also exist, mainly in more forested habitats. Both sexes sport antlers, though they are much bigger in males.

TRACKS Hoof-prints are crescent-shaped cleaves that leave distinctive, almost round imprints with sharp edges. The dew claws are placed low on the legs, so they almost always leave prints. Male prints are larger than those of the female, with fore-prints typically 8–9cm long and 10cm wide. Hind-prints are slightly narrower.

DROPPINGS In summer Reindeer usually produce watery, pale brown droppings of between 1 and 1.5cm long and 1cm wide. In winter, droppings are more solid, pellet-like and dark chocolate brown.

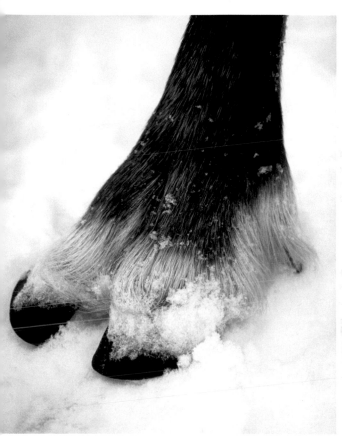

Above: The Reindeer hoof is broad and the cleaves well splayed.

Left: Wild Forest Reindeer in Finland. Although their hooves have evolved for wintry conditions, Reindeer still struggle in deep snow and then become easier targets for large predators.

Elk
Alces alces

Known in North America as the Moose, the Elk is Europe's largest deer. Bull Elk often stand over 2m, and their long legs enable them to traverse boggy ground in summer and snow in winter. Elk inhabit wet forests, tree-dotted marshes and floodplains in the north of Europe. They are the most amphibious of Europe's deer, browsing on aquatic plants, saplings, tree bark and other vegetation.

TRACKS Elk hoof-prints are the biggest of all European deer (up to 16cm long and 11cm wide for the hind-hoof of mature bulls). Only those of the biggest Red Deer stags approach these in size. However, unlike those of Red Deer, the dew claws of Elk almost always leave marks, particularly those on the front feet. Those on the hind feet can be set far back from the main cleave-print and so are absent on hard ground. Older Elk leave rounder cleave marks than younger animals, which leave more pointed marks. The overall imprint is rather triangular.

Above: The Elk is by far the biggest deer species in Europe.

Above: An Elk trail through a peat bog in Estonia. This is a regular and well-trodden path.

Right: Elk hoof-print in wet mud in Estonia. Even in this indistinct print, the dew claw marks are clear.

135

Above: Elk droppings in Finland. This pile has been on the ground some time, as the sprouting grass indicates.

DROPPINGS Fresh Elk droppings resemble cocktail chipolatas. They are moist, pale brown, oval or pellet-shaped, slightly tapered at one end and are often in neat piles. Old droppings are drier and paler. At 2–3cm long and 1.5–2cm thick, they are bigger than those of Red Deer. Elk also void more dung-like, rounder, softer droppings, similar to Wild Boar.

OTHER SIGNS Elk gnaw and eat tree bark in winter, when shoots and other vegetation are in short supply, leaving scars. Elk prefer the bark of young pine trees, though in harsh times spruce bark will also be eaten.

Right: Tree gnawed by Elk in Estonia. The bark around the wound has started to heal and the tree will not die.

Above: Elk tooth marks on a tree in Estonia. Besides their size, the height of such marks betrays which deer species was responsible.

Antlers

Only deer have antlers; domestic cattle, sheep, goats and wild ungulates such as Chamois and bison have horns. In most cases only males (stags and bucks) have antlers and the older and bigger the male, the bigger the antlers. The exceptions are Reindeer (both sexes have antlers) and Roe Deer (some females have small prongs). Antlers are formed by fast-growing tissue that covers a hard bony core and are shed each year before a new pair grows (horns are not shed and do not grow anew each year). Each new pair is bigger, with more prongs and points than the previous ones. At first, antlers are full of blood vessels and nerves and coated in a furry skin called velvet. This soon peels off and the process is accelerated by the animal rubbing against trees and swishing in vegetation (fraying). The shed velvet is often eaten. Antlers begin to grow in early spring, are used in the rut (battles between males) in the autumn and then dropped soon after. Both antlers may be lost at the same time, or separately, one remaining for a while on 'unicorn' males. Late autumn into winter is a good time to look for antlers.

Roe Deer have small antlers, usually with two or three prongs, which continue to grow through the winter months, lose their velvet in spring and are shed in the late autumn after the rut. Antlers vary in appearance but usually have three pointed prongs on each antler. Yearlings may have six points on their antlers, but most have a pair of single, short spikes. Red Deer antlers vary greatly in size and design, though they never have a flat-palmed area. Those on stags in eastern Europe, for example, are bigger than those in the UK. This is related to climate, habitat, food and genetics. The biggest, oldest stags, aged around 10 years, can have over 30 points, though most have fewer than that, and the bases of the antlers are thick, with the upper points thin. Yearling stags usually have a pair of knobs or their first prongs. Fallow Deer have palmate antlers when fully mature, usually in their fourth year. Some bucks have points known as 'spellers' around their plates, while others will never have full flat plates. Yearlings have single prongs or just short knobs, depending on how well they have fed. Second-year animals have two or three prongs and third-year bucks show the first signs of flat plates. Reindeer have branched antlers and the males have a small, flat area below the tip. Elk bulls typically have palmate antlers, though some individuals may have antlers that lack the flat palm.

Above: Shed Roe Deer antler in Hungary.

Above: Shed Red Deer antler in Hungary.

Above: Fallow Deer antlers in the Czech Republic. The flat palm increases in size as bucks get older – these belong to a mature stag.

BIRDS

Around 600 species of bird regularly occur in Europe, living in every kind of habitat on the land, as well as the sea and, of course, the sky. Due to the great diversity of species and the varied lifestyles they lead, birds leave a rich array of tracks and signs.

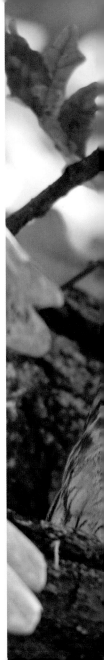

Right: In central and eastern Europe Long-eared Owl *Asio otus* winter roosts can number dozens, sometimes hundreds, of individuals. Hungary.

FEATHERS

Each individual bird has thousands of different feathers on its body, ranging from tiny plumes of fluffy down to sturdy flight feathers and, in some species, long tail feathers. Many feathers are drab, some brightly coloured, but all are moulted at some stage, so it is perhaps not surprising that feathers are one of the most frequently found and recognisable field signs that birds leave.

Above: Waxwing *Bombycilla garrulus* feathers in Hungary. This bird was probably killed and plucked by a hawk, though no body is present. Note the yellow-tipped tail feathers and the red-tipped secondary feather, the so-called 'wax'.

Left: Eagle Owl *Bubo bubo* feathers in Hungary. It is unclear what happened here as there is no corpse and this species has few predators.

Above: The wing of a Eurasian Jay *Garrulus glandarius* in Austria. The blue and black barred coverts are unmistakable.

Above: Avocet *Recurvirostra avosetta* feathers in Hungary. The top feather has been bitten off just before the tip by a predator, perhaps a Fox or Stoat. The lower feather (taken from the same carcass and shown here for comparison) was not bitten and still has its pointed shaft tip.

Above: A Great Bustard *Otis tarda* feather in the snow in Hungary.

Above: Common Crane *Grus grus* feathers are easy to identify. They can be found at places where these large birds congregate during migration, such as this site in Hungary.

Above: Little Owl *Athene noctua* feathers are usually easier to find inside buildings like this one in Hungary than outside in the country.

Above: The feathers of Eurasian Griffon Vulture *Gyps fulvus* are usually unmistakable. They can be found at places where these huge birds moult, like this one in the Spanish Pyrenees, and around carcasses.

FOOTPRINTS

The most frequently found bird footprints are those belonging to species that spend much time on the ground. These include larger species such as geese, grouse and bustards, but also those that stand in mud or sand, like herons, gulls, terns and shorebirds.

Above: A Common Crane *Grus grus* footprint in Estonia. The three broad toes and clear mark of the hind metatarsal are typical.

Above: Greylag Geese *Anser anser* footprints in wet sand in Estonia. The concave webbing between the toes, which is typical for wildfowl, does not show well here.

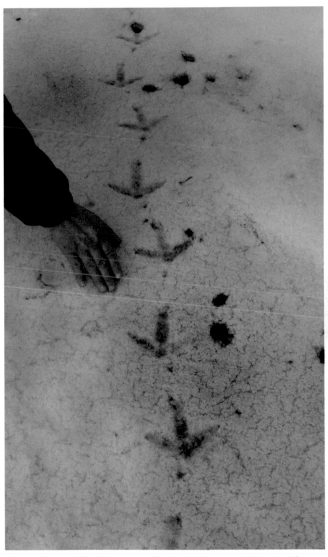

Above: Capercaillie *Tetrao urogallus* tracks in snow in Estonia. The closeness of the prints indicates a bird walking at a slow pace.

Above: A Grey Heron *Ardea cinerea* footprint in light snow on a road in Hungary.

Above: A Great Bustard *Otis tarda* footprint in sand in Hungary. The very fine sand has resulted in an ill-defined print, but the three large toes and a heel print can be seen.

Above: Mallard *Anas platyhynchos* footprints in ice in Hungary. This seemingly haphazard maze of tracks is typical for ducks.

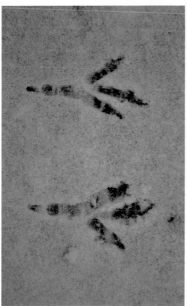

Left: Hooded Crow *Corvus cornix* footprints in Hungary. The paired feet reflect the usual hopping gait.

DROPPINGS

Many birds produce faeces that are too liquid and too temporary to find and accurately identify. Those that are discovered can sometimes be placed in a family, but few if any droppings are diagnostic to one species. White wash on coastal boulders shows where birds such as cormorants and gulls have roosted and splashes on inland cliffs betray the nesting sites of vultures, crows and owls that would otherwise go unnoticed. The droppings of birds in the grouse family are amongst those most often found, as they are relatively solid and durable and left on the ground.

Left: Droppings of Capercaillie *Tetrao urogallus* in Spain. Europe's biggest grouse produces cigarette-sized droppings that vary in colour. A pile can resemble the emptied contents of an ashtray.

Left: Droppings of Hazel Grouse *Bonasa bonasia* in Slovakia resemble old cigarette butts in shape and size. The white areas are urine caps.

Above: Dropping of a Rock Partridge *Alectoris graeca* in Croatia. This dropping is moist and very fresh, still retaining the green colour of the plants eaten.

Above: Droppings of Ptarmigan *Lagopus muta* in Spain. These are typical grouse droppings, being cylindrical and mainly composed of vegetation.

Above: Droppings of Greylag Goose *Anser anser* in Hungary. The upper droppings are dark and moist and therefore new, whilst the lower dropping is pale and dry and hence old. The large area of dried white urine is typical for geese.

Above: The splash of White Stork *Ciconia ciconia* droppings and sticks on the road below a nest in Hungary.

Left: Long-eared Owl *Asio otus* droppings and pellets in Serbia. Such masses of white splash, droppings and pellets often points to a winter roost of owls in the trees above.

Above: Barn Owl *Tyto alba* droppings and food remains, mostly of bats, in an attic in Hungary.

Above: Wood Pigeon *Columba palumbus* dropping in Hungary. Many birds deposit soft but intact droppings like this, with attached white urine paste but no clear contents. Size and location help in identification. The greenish colour indicates that the diet was mainly plant matter.

PELLETS

Many kinds of birds regurgitate food remains that they cannot digest in the form of pellets. Herons, storks, crows, gulls, birds of prey and owls, for example, all expel matter in this way. Pellets differ in size, shape, colour and contents, depending upon the species and what has been eaten. Owls in particular have been the subjects of studies on pellet contents, with favoured prey identified from the fur, bone and skull fragments they contain. Some birds drop pellets whenever the need arises, while others seem to wait until they are at their regular roost, and piles accumulate on the ground at such sites. Where birds roost communally, large mounds of many pellets and droppings can be conspicuous.

Above: Barn Owl *Tyto alba* pellets and feathers in Serbia. The pellets of this species are typically the roundest of all European owls and often quite dark and solid. These examples were 4cm long.

Above: Eagle Owl *Bubo bubo* pellet in Spain. Europe's largest owl naturally coughs up the biggest pellets. This dark example is 9cm long, though over 10cm is common. Contents vary greatly from region to region, reflecting the locally abundant prey.

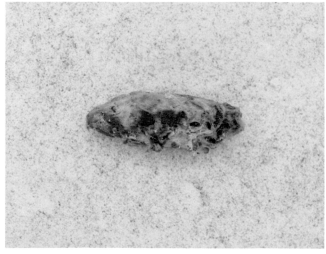

Above: A Snowy Owl *Bubo scandiacus* pellet. This pale example, reflecting the colour of the mammal or bird prey eaten, is 6cm long.

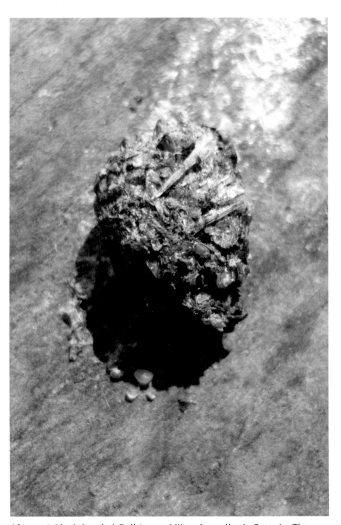

Above: A Black-headed Gull *Larus ridibundus* pellet in Estonia. The pellets of this species are spherical rather than cylindrical and the colour and contents vary greatly according to diet. This pellet is heart-shaped (3cm long and 2cm wide) and brittle, being a delicate mixture of fish bones and other marine prey matter. They are regurgitated at random.

Above: Pellets of Long-eared Owl *Asio otus* in the Czech Republic. Though almost always long and slender, these four examples (from 3 to 4cm long) illustrate the variation that can exist.

Above: Bee-eater *Merops apiaster* pellets in Hungary. These are dry and brittle, being composed of undigested insect fragments. Colour depends upon which prey has been eaten. The complete pellet is around 2cm long. They are found below frequently used perches.

NESTS

Every species of bird has a typical nest type. Nests come in a multitude of sizes, structures and designs. Some are conspicuous and unmistakable, while others are discrete or hidden and not so obvious. Some birds breed in colonies, others alone. Besides size and shape, location also helps in establishing which species made any particular nest, as most species have typical nesting sites. Some nests are very simple – in fact, hardly a nest at all but just a scrape or hollow in the ground (bustards, nightjars and some plovers) or on a cliff ledge (Eagle Owl, Peregrine Falcon and guillemots) with little if any bedding. Some ground-nesting birds (divers, geese, ducks, grouse, partridges, skuas and sea terns) may add a little debris, vegetation or down to their scrape. More substantial nests include untidy masses of sticks (cormorants and herons). Ingenious nests include floating rafts (grebes, coots and marsh terns) that rise and fall with water levels. The most complex nests are usually the easiest ones to identify, such as the hanging home of the Penduline Tit, with its spout entrance, the weaved, enclosed balls of Wren and Long-tailed Tit, and the cemented cup of the House Martin. Of course, many songbirds build open, cupped nests in bushes (thrushes, warblers and finches) or on the ground (larks and pipits). Some of the biggest and most obvious nests are the twig platforms (Osprey, some eagles and White Stork).

Other birds dig burrows in the ground or sandy banks (petrels, shearwaters, puffins, kingfishers, bee-eaters and Sand Martin). Woodpeckers excavate chambers in trees, and entrance holes can be identified to species based on size and shape. Some birds do not make nests at all, but use those made by others. For example, magpie and crow nests are used by small falcons and Long-eared Owls, while sparrows will occupy House Martin nests and even squat inside the huge nests of White Storks. Woodpecker cavities are amongst the most secure and successful nesting sites and are used by many other birds, as well as mammals and insects. Winter is a good season for finding nests in trees, as there is less foliage and, of course, the birds are not breeding so won't be disturbed.

Right: White Storks, such as this one in Serbia, place their huge platform nests of twigs on solid structures such as cliffs, large trees, chimneys and utility poles.

Above: Birds sometimes choose the most unlikely places to build their nests. This White Wagtail *Motacilla alba* nest is in the upper part of a rubbish bin where cigarettes are stubbed out at a Hungarian–Croatian border crossing.

Above: House Martin *Delichon urbica* nests in Hungary. The house owner had placed a shelf below the top row of nests to catch the birds' droppings, but the inventive martins subsequently made another row of nests below the shelf.

Above: House Martin nests used by House Sparrows *Passer domesticus* in the Czech Republic. The original entrance holes have been broken and enlarged by the new occupants.

Left: Some birds readily take to nest boxes, but this is not without risk. The Great Tit *Parus major* nest in this box in Hungary has been robbed. It is unclear which predator is the culprit as there is no clear evidence. A marten or woodpecker is likely, though the former usually leaves claws marks on the box and the latter leaves beak marks around the entrance hole.

FEEDING SIGNS

With so many species foraging in so many ways, there is space here to only briefly touch upon the vast subject of the feeding signs that birds leave.

Above: An acorn wedged in bark by a Eurasian Nuthatch *Sitta europaea* in Hungary. As its name suggests, hacking through nutshells to extract seeds is the usual method used.

Above: Seeds split by Hawfinch *Coccothraustes coccothraustes* in Hungary. Even the hardest seeds are split neatly in two by this species, which has a large, powerful beak.

Above: A Song Thrush *Turdus philomelos* anvil. This bird uses a stone or other hard surface to break open shells before eating the snail inside. Sometimes shells are smashed on the nearest hard place, but regular anvils are also used where piles of broken shells accumulate. This one is at a metal and concrete drain cover in Hungary.

Above: Oystercatcher *Haematopus ostralegus* killed by Peregrine Falcon *Falco peregrinus* in Scotland. The mass of plucked feathers in the open is typical of this large falcon.

WOODPECKERS
Picidae

As a group, woodpeckers are one of the best bird families in terms of the signs they leave. They excavate nesting and roosting chambers in trees, and leave a range of holes, marks and debris when foraging. There are 10 species of true woodpecker in Europe and all hack into trees with their chisel-like bills. Most woodpeckers make several holes every year, mostly in early spring. Some are used as nesting sites, others as roosts, and some are used for both purposes. Many other animals – dormice, squirrels, martens, hornets, bees and many birds – that are unable to excavate their own cavities benefit from this woodpecker work by taking over unused holes. In some cases birds such as the Jackdaw *Corvus monedula* and mammals like Pine Marten actively drive out occupying woodpeckers from their own holes in order to steal and use the cavity. Some woodpeckers create and maintain 'anvils' (also called 'smithies' or 'workshops'). These are cracks or crevices, in trees or walls, where large or hard items, such as pine cones and nuts, are wedged before being hacked open. Regular anvils will have piles of discarded cones on the ground below them. Woodpeckers will also search for prey in man-made wooden structures – behaviour that does not always make them popular.

Above: A Black Woodpecker *Dryocopus martius* has hacked into the wooden door frame of this barn in Spain in search of invertebrates.

Above: A tree stump 'beaten-up' by Black Woodpecker in Estonia in search of invertebrate prey.

Above: A stump shaved by White-backed Woodpecker *Dendrocopos leucotos* in Hungary. In Europe, this foraging method of completely removing all the bark and a thin layer of wood beneath from dead trees is diagnostic.

Above: Black Woodpecker foraging holes in Estonia. Only one European bird is able to excavate large vertical slits like these in trees.

Right: A hole made by a Great Spotted Woodpecker *Dendrocopos major* in a wooden cabin door in Hungary. Woodpeckers that do this are probably in search of hibernating invertebrates, but it is not totally clear why they hack into buildings like this one, which are not rotten and not infested with pests. One theory is that woodpeckers bore into such surfaces because they are deceived into thinking that prey is inside by the sounds made by electricity cables, which resemble the high frequency sounds made by invertebrates.

Above: Bark removed by a Eurasian Three-toed Woodpecker *Picoides tridactylus* in Austria to reach bark beetle larvae. The winding trails left by the burrowing insects can be seen on the exposed surface.

Above: Holes made by Great Spotted Woodpecker in a wooden utility pole in Hungary. These are not nest holes and it is unlikely that any insect prey lies in the timber, as it has been treated, so it is unclear why some woodpeckers do this.

Above: A hole made by a Great Spotted Woodpecker in a fisherman's cabin wall in the Czech Republic.

Above: A utility pole with a woodpecker hole in Hungary. The species is unknown.

Right: A spruce cone fed on by a Great Spotted Woodpecker in Slovakia. The rough, untidy appearance, with scales twisted but not removed, is typical for woodpeckers. Small mammals remove the scales and the cones do not look as battered when feeding is over.

Above: An almond in an anvil. Given the location – a garden in Budapest, Hungary – this could be an anvil of either Great Spotted Woodpecker or Syrian Woodpecker *Dendrocopos syriacus*. The tree is a False Acacia (*Robinia*), which has rugged bark with many suitable crevices in which to wedge items carried from elsewhere.

Above: A pile of cones below a woodpecker anvil in Finland. Once the seeds have been extracted, wedged cones are flicked out or pulled out and dropped.

Above: A conifer cone wedged into an anvil by a Great Spotted Woodpecker in Estonia.

Above: Nutshell debris below an anvil in Hungary. There are cracked almond and walnuts shells of various ages, showing that this anvil is regularly used.

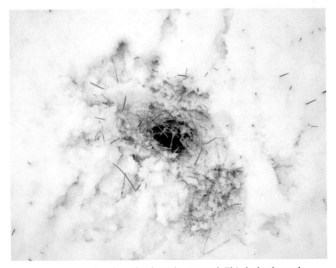

Above: Some woodpeckers feed on the ground. This hole through snow was made by Eurasian Green Woodpecker *Picus viridis*, which is the most terrestrial woodpecker in Europe, to reach prey in the soft soil beneath.

SHRIKE LARDERS

Shrikes (Laniidae) are small to medium-sized songbirds with hooked bills. They are known as 'butcher birds' in folk-English because of their habit of impaling prey such as insects, lizards, rodents and smaller birds on thorns, sharp twigs or barbed wire. It is thought that shrikes do this because they lack the raptor-like talons needed to grip prey and are reluctant to eat it on the ground. However, these sites also seem to function as food larders that can be returned to.

Right: A shrike larder in Hungary. This Chiffchaff *Phylloscopus collybita* has been impaled on a thorn by a Red-backed Shrike *Lanius collurio*. The victim is half eaten and there is a parasitic wasp on the exposed flesh near the thorn.

REPTILES

Reptiles include tortoises, terrapins, lizards, geckos and snakes. Although some reptiles, such as Common Lizard *Zootoca vivipara*, Slow Worm *Anguis fragilis* and Grass Snake *Natrix natrix*, occur over large areas of Europe, the warmer Mediterranean and Balkan countries host the majority of the continent's species. Several species are endemic to small geographical areas, particularly Mediterranean islands. Some lizards and geckos are common and easy to observe in coastal holiday resorts, the latter invariably sticking to walls and ceilings with their adhesive footpads. As a group, reptiles leave relatively few tracks and signs, certainly in comparison to mammals and birds. Some reptiles lay eggs, while others, like the Adder *Vipera berus*, are viviparous, giving birth to live young. Shed skins can sometimes be found, but these are often hard to assign to an exact species.

Right: An Aesculapian Snake *Zamenis longissimus* in Croatia. These snakes are found across southern and central Europe and there is an introduced population in London. They can reach 2m in length and are good tree climbers.

Above: The shed skin of an Aesculapian Snake in Hungary. The location and habitat are important factors when attempting to identify such skin remains, as they are very similar from species to species. This snake occurs from France eastwards to the Black Sea.

Above: The hatched eggs of the Four-lined Snake *Elaphe quatuorlineata* in Italy. This is one of the largest snakes in Europe, often over 2m in length, and occurs in Italy and the Balkans. White, oval eggs of 4–7cm in length are usually laid in rocky crevices. These seem to have hatched successfully, as there are no signs of predation.

Above: Snake droppings in Croatia. The species is unknown, but given the size of the excrement and the location, it is certainly a large urban-dwelling species. Note the tangle of undigested hard remains and fur.

Above: Hatched Turkish Gecko *Hemidactylus turcicus* eggs in Croatia. Also known as the Mediterranean Gecko, this common reptile is at home in rocky areas and on buildings, even inside houses. Two white, round eggs about 1.2cm in diameter are usually laid, and these probably hatched successfully as there are no signs of predation.

Above: These gecko droppings are almost certainly Turkish Gecko or Moorish Gecko *Tarentola mauritanica*, given the location on the Adriatic coast of Croatia. They are pellet-shaped, 1–2cm long, composed of brittle insect remains and crumble easily. The white pellet is dried urine.

INVERTEBRATES

The study of the tracks and signs left by invertebrates (animals that do not have a backbone) is rather neglected. This is perhaps not surprising, as the subject is vast with innumerable, often tiny creatures leaving signs that are often indistinct and impossible to assign to species. One of the most productive habitats to search for such signs is the seashore, particularly in the mud and sand of estuaries. Europe's coastline is home to a wealth of wildlife, with molluscs, crustaceans and worms in particular leaving shells and holes, and other wildlife leaving evidence of how they have eaten these creatures. Inland, the most familiar signs that European terrestrial invertebrates leave include bee and wasp hives, beetle burrows, wasp galls, cocoons and spiders' webs.

Above: The Violet Carpenter Bee *Xylocopa violacea* makes its nest in dead wood. Note the sawdust below this freshly excavated cavity in a rotten post in Hungary.

Right: Honeycomb fragments on the ground in Spain. The beehive was above in a tree hole and the honeycomb was presumably removed by a predator.

WASP GALLS

Certain wasps inject chemicals into plants to induce the growth of galls, where their larvae feed and develop. In Europe, galls are more common on deciduous trees than on conifers, with oaks hosting the most types. So-called oak-apples are round, often lumpy galls, 2–5cm in diameter, found mostly on the underside of leaves and induced by the Oak Apple Gall Wasp *Biorhiza pallida*. Cherry-galls are made to form by the small Black Gall Wasp *Cynips quercusfolii*. These galls, 1.5–2.5cm in diameter, are smooth or rough depending upon the tree they are on, and yellowish or green with a red-pink sheen at first, before turning brown. The fluffy, red and green, mossy growths found on the twigs of wild rose bushes are galls made by the Bedeguar Gall Wasp *Diplolepis rosae*. This tiny wasp lays its eggs in leaf buds and shoots, which react and develop into hard galls covered in fluffy hairs called Robin's Pincushion. The pincushions host around 30–40 offspring that feed on the plant through the winter before emerging the following spring. The galls are pea-sized, and the fluffy hairs can be 3–4cm long.

Above: A Robin's Pincushion gall in Croatia. Like all galls, these are easier to find than the actual wasps that make them.

ANTHILLS

Above: An anthill in Finland. Several species of wood ants build such mounds.

Some species of ant build a dome-shaped mound of conifer needles, plant stems, woodchips, small twigs, leaves and earth debris to cover their colony. These anthills are often based around a tree stump in a sunny, south-facing spot and are instantly recognisable. Woodland ants in the *Formica* genus construct mounds as large as 2m across at the base and 1m high. Clear narrow trails on the ground, made by innumerable tiny feet repeatedly treading back and forth, often run between anthills and feeding places or to other colonies. When closely examined, it can be seen that the materials used on the anthill are not placed haphazardly, but have been precisely arranged by the worker ants to ensure that rain runs off. The southern side of mounds is also flatter, presumably to expose a greater surface area to the sun.

PINE PROCESSIONARY MOTH
Thaumetopoea pityocampa

The Pine Processionary Moth *Thaumetopoea pityocampa* is common in much of southern and eastern Europe. In some years population outbreaks occur and the species is regarded as a pest by foresters, as its caterpillars quickly defoliate trees. Its caterpillars spend the winter in silky nests in the tops of pines and sometimes other trees. These resemble a cluster of spider webs and are called tents. In plague years they are unmissable, with several often placed in the same tree.

Above: A Pine Processionary Moth tent in Croatia. These should not be touched, as the caterpillars are covered in hairs that contain a poison that irritates the skin.

BARK BEETLES

Tunnels and burrows gnawed in the cambium layer of trees by adults and larvae of wood-boring beetles are revealed when bark falls away. These patterns can be both on the trunk and on the underside of the bark. One of the largest European species, the Great Capricorn Beetle *Cerambyx cerdo* makes impressive, finger-sized, often crescent-shaped holes and burrows in mature oak trees. Sawdust accumulates below freshly worked trees. As their names suggest, smaller species such as Spruce Bark Beetle *Hylastes cunicularius*, Large Pine-shoot Beetle *Tomicus piniperda*, Ash Bark Beetle *Hylesinus fraxini*, Large Elm Bark Beetle *Scolytus scolytus* and Oak Bark Beetle *Scolytus intricatus* all specialise in certain trees, with each creating winding patterns under the bark. Typical patterns have a central burrow (the maternal gallery) with numerous side passages running from it in either straight or winding lines. The Engraver Beetle *Ips typographus* creates particularly intricate galleries when tunnelling below the bark of spruce. The Engraver is regarded as a major pest by foresters, its larvae usually working away in the lower and middle sections of trunks. Infested trees have fine reddish-brown dust at the base of their trunks. Panels of fallen bark show these markings on their underside.

Above: An exposed burrow of Great Capricorn Beetle larva in the Czech Republic. The round holes are flight-holes, from where the beetle finally emerged.

Above: An oak tree patterned with the burrows and holes of *Cerambyx* beetles in the Czech Republic. The holes in the bark to the left were made by woodpeckers searching for the insects.

Above: Patterns on the underside of tree bark made by the Engraver Beetle in Austria.

Above: Exposed trails of Large Pine-shoot Beetle larvae on a tree trunk in Slovakia. The single round hole is an exit from where the adult beetle emerged.

ROMAN SNAIL
Helix pomatia

The Roman Snail (also known as the Edible Snail or Escargot) is mainly terrestrial but does climb in bushes and up tree trunks. It is Europe's largest snail and it is common and widespread across much of the continent in areas with lime-rich soils, though rare in Britain. When fully grown, the snails are around 10cm long and live in shells of 4–5cm in diameter. Shells are various shades of buff and brown with 4–5 darker stripes. Whole shells and those cracked or punctured by predators are often easy to find.

Above: A Roman Snail shell probably bitten by a marten or polecat in Hungary. The two holes show where the canines punctured the shell.

Right: Empty Roman Snail shell in Hungary. Undamaged shells like this, with no signs of predation, are commonly found.

ROADKILL AND REMAINS

Though it may be a gruesome subject for some, the presence of some animals in an area is often only revealed when they are found dead. This is especially true for nocturnal animals, which may live amongst us but go undetected until they meet a sad end on roads. The skulls and skeletons of long-dead animals remain long after corpses have decomposed or been eaten. As with roadkill, skulls and bones can reveal that animals that may have gone unnoticed when alive actually occur in an area. A basic knowledge of anatomy, especially dental types, is useful when identifying remains. Questions to answer include whether the animal was a carnivore or herbivore.

Right: Beech Martens *Martes foina* can be common in urban areas but are mostly nocturnal. Their presence is sometimes only revealed when they are found dead by the roadside, such as this one in Hungary.

Above: A Brown Hare *Lepus europaeus* recently hit by a vehicle in Hungary. Despite the devastation, the animal is easily identified by its size, colour and key body parts such as legs and ears.

Above: A long-dead Common Hamster *Cricetus cricetus* in Hungary. Though totally flattened and dried out, the size, shape, colour and location are enough to positively identify the animal.

Above: The remains of a Roe Deer *Capreolus capreolus* in Austria (cause of death unknown). The species can be identified by the overall dimensions and the colour of the leg and hoof.

Above: The skull of a Eurasian Badger *Meles meles* in Hungary. Note the long jawbone and canines.

Above: A Chamois *Rupicapra rupicapra* corpse in Austria. The cause of death is unclear, as there are no signs of predator attack and the body was far from the road. Many Chamois die in winter due to harsh weather and lack of food, so starvation is likely. Note the brown and tan coat and the shiny black hooves.

GLOSSARY

carrion: dead and decaying animal flesh, often eaten by carnivores.

chitin: a tough, protective substance that forms the main component of insect exoskeletons.

cloven-hoof: a hoof that is divided into two digits, for example deer and cattle.

colour morph: a range of colours or shades that may occur in one species, for example in the fur of Red Squirrels and Red Foxes.

crepuscular: animals that are active mainly during twilight (at dawn and dusk).

hibernaculum: the place chosen by an animal for its hibernation.

scat: the name for the droppings of dogs and cats.

spraint: the name for the droppings of otters.

substrate: the surface material, such as mud, gravel or sand, into which a track or print is imprinted.

understorey: plant life that grows beneath the forest canopy.

ORGANISATIONS

Amphibian and Reptile
Conservation Trust (ARC)
http://www.arc-trust.org

British Trust for Ornithology (BTO)
http://www.bto.org

IUCN Europe
http://www.iucn.org/about/union/
secretariat/offices/europe

The Mammal Society
http://www.mammal.org.uk

Tracks & Signs Blog
http://tracksandsigns.blogspot.com

ACKNOWLEGEMENTS

The majority of photographs in this book are my own, but I would like to
thank the following for the use of their photographs: Daniel Alder, Botond
Bako, Sandor Boldogh, Michael Crutch, Julian Gayarre Igazuirre, Jozsef Serfozo,
Dominic Boyer and Kari Kemppainen of Boreal Wildlife, Finland.
Thanks are also due to Laszlo Albert, Simon Cook and Andras Schmidt.
Special thanks to Jane Lawes, Simon Papps and Sally McFall.

IMAGE CREDITS

Bloomsbury Publishing would like to thank the following for providing
photographs.

12 Sandor Boldogh; 13 (bottom) Daniel Alder; 14–15 Jozsef Serfozo; 17 Kari
Kemppainen; 20 Shutterstock; 22 Shutterstock; 27 Sandor Boldogh; 28–29
Sandor Boldogh; 30 Sandor Boldogh; 31 Sandor Boldogh; 32 Shutterstock; 34
Shutterstock; 40 Shutterstock; 42 Shutterstock; 45 (top) Shutterstock; 45
(bottom) Botond Bako; 46 Shutterstock; 50 Shutterstock; 52 Shutterstock;
54 Shutterstock; 56 Shutterstock; 62 Shutterstock; 64 Shutterstock; 68
Shutterstock; 70 Kari Kemppainen; 72–73 Kari Kemppainen; 74 Shutterstock;
75 (top) Julian Gayarre Igazuirre; 76 Shutterstock; 77 Julian Gayarre
Igazuirre; 78 Shutterstock; 80 Shutterstock; 82 Shutterstock; 84
Shutterstock; 86 Shutterstock; 89 (bottom) Michael Crutch; 90 Kari
Kemppainen; 91 Kari Kemppainen; 92–93 Dominic Boyer; 94 Shutterstock; 96
Shutterstock; 98 Julian Gayarre Igazuirre; 99 Shutterstock; 100–101 Kari
Kemppainen; 101 (top) Shutterstock; 110 Shutterstock; 114 Shutterstock;
118 Shutterstock; 120–121 Kari Kemppainen; 122 Shutterstock; 126
Shutterstock; 130 Shutterstock; 132 Kari Kemppainen; 133 Shutterstock; 134
Shutterstock; 150 (top) Julian Gayarre Igazuirre; 151 (top right) Julian
Gayarre Igazuirre; 153 (top) Sandor Boldogh; 163 (bottom) Michael Crutch.

INDEX